THE A-Z OF CURIOUS
BRISTOL

First published 2014

The History Press
The Mill, Brimscombe Port
Stroud, Gloucestershire, GL5 2QG
www.thehistorypress.co.uk

British Library Cataloguing in Publication Data.
A catalogue record for this book is available from the British Library.

ISBN 978 0 7509 5605 5

Typesetting and origination by The History Press
Printed in Great Britain

Introduction

Strange and fascinating stories abound in Bristol. Perhaps that's not so unusual with a city that has a rich and colourful history stretching back 1,000 years. It is a city of famous churches, famous inns and hidden treasures. There are also quirky customs, archaic practices and ceremonies with origins that baffle not only newcomers to the city but even seasoned Bristolians.

Stroll the city's streets and you may well meet the vicar who once a year goes on a trek to peer down manholes or the girls in red who hold up the city traffic as they pay tribute to a benefactor who survived an attack on his life.

In this book there are also stories from the city's lesser-known history. You can discover why rubble from buildings bombed during the Bristol Blitz was shipped to New York and why a public clock still tells Bristol Time long after Greenwich Mean Time came into common usage.

Then there are the curious and extraordinary characters like the woman who tricked people into believing that she was a princess from an exotic Eastern island, the teacher who invented a thrashing machine to punish errant schoolboys, the 'demon barber' who went over the Niagara Falls in a custom-made beer barrel and the man who joined a tiger in his cage as part of a sales gimmick. Needless to say, neither of the latter lived to tell the tale.

But it's not just human beings who walk through the pages of this book. There's also a Jack Russell terrier that became a worldwide landmark. And then there's the cat who sat next to the church organist during services. You just couldn't make up stories like these, could you?

Maurice Fells, 2014

Acknowledgements

Much of the information for this book has been collected by me over a number of years as a broadcast and print journalist with a passion for the colourful history of my native city. Old newspaper cuttings and press releases that I have kept have been put to good use in the pages of this book.

But there have been forays into the archives of Bristol Reference Library and Bristol Records Office. I am grateful to the staff of both organisations for the remarkable tolerance and patience they have showed in dealing with my numerous enquiries.

Thanks are due also to Mildred and Francis Ford for the use of postcards from their private collection. Grateful thanks are extended to Declan Flynn of The History Press for his support and guidance.

Last, but definitely not least, I express sincere thanks to Janet and Trevor Naylor, who spent much time strolling around the streets of Bristol to capture the many photographic shots that enhance the quality of this book. I owe a big debt of gratitude to Janet for her encouragement and enthusiasm, which pushed me to complete this book.

A

❧ ALE CONNORS' TASTY TASK ❧

In the sixteenth century the council employed two people to do a job that many a beer-lover would envy today. The work of the Ale Connors, as they were officially titled, involved visiting the growing number of breweries in the town.

Their task was to taste the ale that was being brewed to make sure it was wholesome for sale. For this they were paid £2 13s a year. The Ale Connors were required to tell the council about any 'knavish brewers' so that action could be taken against them.

It is not known for certain when brewing started in the town. However, one of the earliest breweries was owned by Sir John Hawkins, Mayor of Bristol, in 1701. The following year he brewed a celebration ale to mark the visit of Queen Anne to the city.

The best known of the breweries was Georges & Co., founded in the 1770s. When the firm decided to become a public company a century later, it caused much excitement in the city. The directors, issuing the prospectus for Bristol Brewery, Georges & Co., intended to keep the subscription list open for a week. But to their astonishment the £400,000 they asked for was oversubscribed on the first day. Within hours the public had offered a staggering £6,300,000.

The brewing industry had gained such a reputation by 1793 that an entry in Matthews' Bristol Directory stated that 'the breweries are numerous and extensive, and their malt liquors are cheaper, finer and better here than in most other towns'. The writer went on say that 'good ale is universally sold for three pence a quart and Burton, a strong beer, for four pence. There is a large porter-brewery in Bath Street which succeeds well in rivalling London porter and meets with great encouragement.'

Eighty years later the directory listed more than two dozen breweries, supplying 1,008 'public houses and beer houses'. The list started with the Adam & Eve on

Hope Chapel Hill, Hotwells, which was first registered in 1775, although it was probably dispensing ale long before that. The pub is still trading today and, unlike many others, it seems that it has never changed its name.

In a passageway leading off Corn Street is the only inn remaining from the fourteen that the city fathers authorised in 1606. However, the history of The Rummer goes back much further. An inn has stood on the same site in All Saints Lane since 1241 when it went by the name of the Greene Lattis, after the lattice work that decorated its exterior.

Alcohol was not only available in pubs, alehouses, taverns, or call them what you will. In the seventeenth century the gaoler at Newgate Prison – the Galleries shopping centre now stands on the site – was ordered by the city fathers to keep a stock of beer on the premises for the consumption of prisoners and their visitors. Any inmate who got drunk was fined £2.

A local paper reported that an 'expert tapster' was wanted by the prison. He would be under the 'protection of The Keeper from all harms and insults'. The prison's tap house was said to be profitable as prisoners and their visitors were allowed to drink as much as they could pay for. It was said that before an execution the prison was crowded with 'bibulous sympathisers'.

❧ ARSONIST WHO TRIED TO BURN BRISTOL DOWN ❧

The man who was wandering around the centre of Bristol late on a cold winter's night in 1777 had the most bizarre and improbable scheme on his mind. James Hill was intent on burning down the town, starting with the docks.

Hill, who had been a highwayman complete with pistols and mask before arriving in Bristol, started to put his plan into action at midnight. He began by spreading turpentine, resin and pitch on the ship *Savannah la Mar* which was being loaded for a journey to Jamaica. The vessel caught alight fairly quickly and Hill then set fire to *La Fame* and *Hibernia*, which were berthed nearby.

The next morning Hill, also known as James Hind, James Aitken but more commonly as Jack the Painter, had the gall to mingle with people looking at the destruction and damage he had caused. The *Savannah* was badly burnt but the fires on the other two ships were spotted quickly and put out.

Hill, who was 25 years old, was back at the quayside again that night, trying to set alight barrels of oil, but this time his attempts at arson fizzled out. He then turned his attention to destroying warehouses near his lodgings in The Pithay. Being of timber construction, the buildings quickly caught alight. In one night, six premises in Bell Lane were destroyed.

A big search for Hill, who had quickly left town, was soon underway. Bristol Corporation offered a £500 reward for information leading to his arrest.

The government put up a further £1,000 reward. A description of Hill appeared on hoardings and he was eventually arrested at Dover after breaking into a shop.

He was taken to Winchester Gaol, where over the next three days he dictated a confession to the Keeper of Prison. In it he admitted fire-raising at dockyards in Chatham, Plymouth, Portsmouth and Bristol.

Less than two months later, his trial on charges of arson took place in the castle at Winchester before two judges, the Honourable Sir William Ashurst and Sir Beaumont Hotham. The court heard that Hill wanted to destroy English commerce.

In passing sentence, the judges ordered that he should be hanged. So it was that a couple of days later that a mizzenmast was taken down from a ship at Portsmouth Dockyard and set up inside Victory Gate. Hill was hanged from this at a height of 60ft. Many thousands of people gathered outside the gate to watch Hill's last moments of life.

❧ ASHTON COURT IMPOSTOR ❧

The stranger who called at Ashton Court Mansion was unceremoniously bundled out of the entrance hall by a servant and dumped in the drive after he claimed to be the long-lost heir to the Smyth family and their estates.

Ashton Court Mansion (Trevor Naylor)

Undeterred, the visitor, who called himself Sir Richard Smyth, pressed on with his claim and took the family to court. The story that unfolded at Gloucester Assize was one of the most bizarre ever to be heard in a court of law.

Mr Justice Coleridge, sitting with a special jury, heard the claimant's extraordinary tale. He insisted that his father was Sir Hugh Smyth, a former owner of Ashton Court who had died about thirty years previously. His mother, he said, was the daughter of a count and had been married to his father at a secret ceremony in Ireland. As a child he had been given to a labouring family in Warminster, Wiltshire, to be brought up.

The claimant also alleged that another member of the Smyth family, Sir Greville Smyth, had privately acknowledged his claim as heir but died suddenly the day afterwards from the shock of it all.

There was a dramatic turn in the court proceedings when a witness identified the would-be-heir to Ashton Court from various marks on his face and hands as Tom Provis, a convicted horse thief.

Provis faced another setback when a telegram arrived at court from a jeweller who had read a report of the previous day's proceedings in *The Times*. The jeweller said that some items of jewellery that Provis claimed to be family heirlooms had been engraved by him just a few months earlier.

Provis also tripped up when, in his ignorance, he misquoted the Smyth family motto. There was also a little discrepancy regarding a date which he could not explain to the court.

After hearing all the evidence, the court decided that Provis' claim to the Smyth estate was false. On Mr Justice Coleridge's warrant he was immediately committed to another court to face a charge of perjury. A further charge of forgery was subsequently added. Provis, still claiming to be Sir Richard Smyth, was convicted on both charges and sentenced to twenty years' transportation. He died in Dartmoor Prison less than two years later, while waiting to be transported.

People living in various parts of the world were gripped by the details of the two court cases. The *Herald and Telegram* in New Zealand told its readers that the case was based on 'a tissue of falsehoods and forgeries sustained by Provis in the witness box'. In England some newspapers even produced supplements about the court hearings.

The Smyth family had lived at Ashton Court, in Long Ashton parish, on the southern edge of Bristol since 1545 when the house was bought by John Smyth. He was one-time mayor of the city and a wealthy merchant engaged in trade with Spain and France, exporting various items including cloth and lead from the Mendip mines in return for wine and dyestuffs.

Various generations of the family added cottages and large estates in Long Ashton to the Smyth property portfolio, either through purchase or marriage. By the time of Provis' claim the Smyth family was collecting about £30,000 a year in rental income from tenants; a small fortune in Victorian times.

The Dovecote, which for more than 150 years traded as the Smyth Arms and was part of the Ashton Court estate (Trevor Naylor)

Down the centuries the family altered and extended the mansion so that it is almost impossible to work out the original plans, although a house on the site can be traced back to 1282. Today, the most notable feature of the house is the long façade of the south front built in two different styles.

When Esme Smyth, the last of the family, died in 1946, there were death duties of nearly £1 million to pay. More than 2,000 acres of the greater estate were sold off including farms, cottages and two pubs, The Angel and the Smyth Arms. Both are still trading today, although the Smyth Arms is now called The Dovecote.

The Smyth Arms dates back to 1578, when it was known as the Coach and Horses. Pints of ale were pulled seven days a week until Sir Greville Smyth was abused while making his way to church by some customers the worse for drink. He used his powers as a Justice of the Peace and revoked the pub's licence. Sir Greville restored it on condition that in future the pub didn't open on Sundays.

About this time its name was changed to honour the Smyth family. When Esme Smyth died, the pub was sold to George's Bristol Brewery, still with its six-day licence.

Mrs Smyth's heir was her grandson, 19-year-old Greville Adrian Cavendish, who was serving in the navy. He decided that taking over the house would be impracticable for him. Ashton Court Mansion and 840 acres of woodland, undulating parkland and ornamental gardens fell into dereliction until it was acquired by Bristol City Council in 1960 at a cost of £103,200.

The estate is probably now best known for hosting the annual Bristol International Balloon Fiesta, which attracts around half a million balloonists and spectators from around the world.

B

❧ BANKING CRASH ❧

As Bristol grew in international importance as a major port and commercial centre, banks in the city flourished too. The first one opened in Corn Street in 1750, where it issued its own notes. It was the first banking house outside London, except for a Jewish-run bank in Derby. By 1900 Bristolians were spoilt for choice, with thirty-five different banks offering them financial services.

One of the biggest was the West of England and South Wales Bank, which had its main office in The Exchange, Corn Street, and forty-seven branches in the two regions.

As business grew the bank needed larger premises and bought the old Bush Inn opposite The Exchange. It was at the Bush that Mr Winkle took up his quarters in his 'love-lorn quest' for the missing Arabella Allen in Charles Dickens' *Pickwick Papers*.

The bank paid £10,000 for the inn, which was demolished, and new headquarters were promptly built on the site. No expense seems to have been spared. The building was designed in an opulent Venetian style, copying St Mark's Library, Venice. An intricate frieze was carved along the length of its façade, representing various commercial activities including the printing of bank notes. The new headquarters opened in 1857.

Towards the end of 1878 rumours were circulating that the bank was unstable. Its directors refuted all the allegations saying that their accounts were in good order. They did say they were hoping to restructure the business. The rumours were not without foundation, for a couple of weeks before Christmas, the directors suspended all payments.

A liquidator was appointed and his report revealed that when the bank crashed, all its paid up capital and a reserve fund of £156,000 had 'entirely disappeared'. Against liabilities of about £350,000, there was a further deficiency of assets exceeding £300,000. The bank's failure was attributed to 'imprudent advances' made over the years to iron firms in South Wales.

Early in 1879, the Home Secretary ordered a prosecution against the bank's chairman Jerome Murch, a former Mayor of Bristol. Sitting alongside him in the dock at the Assize Courts were five of his directors. At the end of their trial the jury acquitted all the defendants.

Lloyds Bank took over the building, which it occupied until January 2014, when it moved the branch to Cabot Circus. As a listed building, the Corn Street site cannot be demolished or have its architectural style changed.

❧ BODYSNATCHERS AT WORK ❧

The body of a young man who was taken to the gallows nearly 200 years ago for killing his girlfriend played a major part in early medical research at Bristol Infirmary.

The infirmary was founded after seventy-eight eminent citizens promised charitable services 'for the benefit of the poor sick'. They pledged between two and six guineas each. However, the generosity of some supporters far exceeded that. One William Clarke donated ten guineas at the original subscription meeting, while the Earl of Hopetoun promised £400 over twenty-five years. Various trade groups from bakers to innkeepers were also approached for financial support.

Their donations meant that a disused brewery building on Lower Maudlin Street could be converted into an infirmary. It treated its first outpatients in May 1737 and in December of that year inpatients were admitted for the first time. It was then that an official opening ceremony for the infirmary was held, followed by a church service. Afterwards one of the surgeons wrote: 'We finished the day amidst the smoke of tobacco and emptying and replenishing of mugs of Bristol ale.'

Initially operations took place in the wards, until the infirmary's first dedicated theatre opened in 1755. Almost 100 years later, Queen Victoria granted the infirmary the right to call itself 'Royal'.

In the early part of the nineteenth century there was a demand from surgeons for bodies for dissection so that knowledge of anatomy could be passed on to their students.

Richard Smith, who was the infirmary's senior surgeon from 1796 until his death in 1843, acquired the body of the first person to be hanged at the city's New Gaol. He had the skin of John Horwood tanned and dressed, and used it to bind a book that contains details of his court trial and information about the dissection. The cover of the book is inscribed in Latin with the words 'Cutis vera Johannus Horwood'. Translated, this means 'the actual skin of John Horwood'. What may be seen as a rather macabre book is now in the care of Bristol Records Office.

Horwood's skeleton hung in a cupboard at the University of Bristol's medical school until recently, when it was claimed by his descendants who organised a funeral for him.

As the demand for bodies for research grew, so did the activities of 'grave robbers' (or 'body resurrectionists', as they were called). In February 1828 a local paper reported that 'two grave robbers' were caught trying to open a tomb in Brislington churchyard. Doctors Wallis and Riley were each fined £6. However, Dr Wallis's appearance before the magistrates does not seem to have hampered his career prospects at the infirmary. A few weeks after his court case, the same magistrates proposed that he should be elected to the post of physician at the hospital.

On another occasion it was reported that several doctors were found in Bedminster churchyard, about to begin their 'nefarious work of plundering a grave' where a body had been interred a few days earlier. The medical men were about to raise the body when the local constable on beat duty caught them in the act. They too, had an appointment with the magistrates.

Following a similar incident at St Augustine's Abbey, which later evolved into Bristol Cathedral, the churchwarden made a special announcement. He offered a reward of fifty guineas for information 'leading to the conviction of the person or persons who removed the corpse of a female interred in the churchyard the previous day'.

The Bristol Royal Infirmary was the first hospital outside of London to be supported by voluntary contributions. For many years the hospital had to find different ways of raising funds to enable its doctors to give their services free of charge to the poor.

Under the presidency of Sir George White, the sum of £7,500 was raised by a week-long carnival in 1905 at the Zoological Gardens in Clifton. On the last day of the event Sir George, a prominent local stockbroker, industrialist and philanthropist, added the sum of £7,500 from his own pocket, wiping out the infirmary's debt of £15,000.

The infirmary continues to treat the sick, search for cures for diseases, and teach medical students.

❧ BRIDGING THE GAP ❧

When he died in 1754 Alderman William Vick, a wealthy wine merchant, left £1,000 in his will towards the cost of building a bridge to span the Avon Gorge, linking Leigh Woods on the Somerset side with Clifton on the Bristol side. Vick left instructions that the money should be invested until it had reached £10,000, a sum that he thought would be enough to carry out his wish. In the event, the bridge cost almost ten times that amount and the extra money needed was raised in shares.

In his will Vick also said that on his bridge 'the passage was to be free from toll'. This request was enshrined in a Clifton Suspension Bridge Act of Parliament, but

Looking down the River Avon to the Clifton Suspension Bridge (Trevor Naylor)

it seems to have been forgotten long ago. It's now more unlikely than ever that the tolls motorists pay to cross the bridge will be dropped, because of the rising costs of its upkeep.

Isambard Kingdom Brunel, who designed the bridge, described it as 'my first child, my darling'. His original plan included two giant sphinxes on the top of the towers at each end of the bridge, but the cost was prohibitive.

Although construction work started in 1831, it was dogged by financial problems and the bridge was not finished until 1864. Just seven years after starting work the contractors became bankrupt and everything came to a halt. Another firm was found to take over but in 1843 funds ran out and work temporarily stopped again. The time allowed by an Act of Parliament for the bridge completion expired in May 1853. A new firm, the Clifton Suspension Bridge Company, was formed and another Act of Parliament obtained. Eventually the bridge was completed as a memorial to Brunel who, unfortunately, had died five years before its opening.

There was much excitement in the city when the bridge was officially opened amidst much pomp and ceremony on 8 December 1864. Bristol had never seen anything like it. A mile-long procession of tradesmen carrying banners and flags made its way from the city centre to Clifton. The city's great and good were joined on a specially built grandstand by Members of Parliament, as well as civic dignitaries from Somerset who were there as part of the bridge stands in their county. Church bells rang, bands played and guns fired salutes as the Lords Lieutenant of Gloucestershire and Somerset officially declared the bridge open.

The first member of the public to cross the bridge was 21-year-old Mary Griffiths, of Hanham. She ran across the 702ft span to make sure no one beat her.

Clifton Suspension Bridge spanning the Avon Gorge (Trevor Naylor)

The next day *The Times* reported that 'a large muster of gentlemen, who came in uniform of some kind or other, made upon the whole, a very brilliant show, worthy both of the place and the occasion'. It was estimated that 100,000 people gathered on the roads and grass slopes around the bridge to watch the proceedings.

Brunel, who designed the bridge in the days of the horse and cart, could hardly have envisaged that 150 years later it would be carrying around 3.5 million cars a year. Many motorists who cross from the Leigh Woods side are probably unaware that they are driving up a slight incline. The Clifton end of the bridge is 3ft higher than the other side. Brunel designed it that way to create a level appearance, because of the topography of the area.

It is very rare for anyone to survive a fall from the bridge, 245ft above the high water level of the River Avon. However, in 1885 Sarah Ann Henley, aged 22, threw herself off it after being jilted by her lover. She was saved by her billowing skirt, which acted as a parachute. Sarah went on to live until she was 84 years old.

Eleven years later, 3-year-old Elsie Brown and her sister Ruby, aged 12, were thrown off the bridge by their father. However, a strong wind and a high tide helped to break their fall.

Clifton Suspension Bridge has always been seen as a challenge to pilots who want to fly over or under it. Frenchman Maurice Tetard had the distinction in 1910 of being the first person to fly over the bridge. He was demonstrating a Bristol Boxkite aircraft made by the British and Colonial Aircraft Company at Filton.

Sadly, an attempt by Flying Officer John Crossley to fly under the bridge in 1957 ended in tragedy. The 27-year-old lost his life as he attempted a barrel roll in a de Havilland Vampire jet after going under the bridge. His aircraft crashed into the Leigh Woods side of the Avon Gorge and burst into flames.

❧ BRUNEL'S OTHER BRIDGE ❧

Lying almost in the shadow of the Clifton Suspension Bridge is Brunel's much lesser known tubular swing, or swivel, bridge. It was operating in 1849, fifteen years before his much grander structure, airily spanning the Avon Gorge, was completed.

This was Brunel's first tubular wrought-iron swing bridge and originally carried traffic over the south entrance lock of the Cumberland Basin. It was later shortened and moved to the lock at the north entrance to the basin. The bridge was designed by staff working in Brunel's office in Westminster but he closely monitored both the planning and construction of the bridge.

Its original turning machinery was a hand-turned crank. This was later changed to a hydraulic system running on fresh water that came from a pressured water system in the nearby Underfall Yard.

After almost 120 years of service, the bridge was decommissioned in 1968. This was brought about by the opening of the Cumberland Basin flyover and swing bridge complex.

Brunel's Other Bridge (Trevor Naylor)

The bridge now lies abandoned partly under the Cumberland Basin flyover (Trevor Naylor)

The tubular bridge now lies abandoned on the dockside, partly hidden beneath the flyover. Its future is unknown, although several environmental groups are campaigning to get it restored; so far, without success. English Heritage has, however, recognised the bridge as a 'building at risk'.

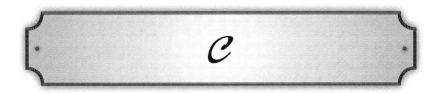

C

⚜ CHURCH ON THE MOVE ⚜

St Werburgh's church once stood on the corner of Small Street and Corn Street but towards the end of the nineteenth century, the Church of England decided to move it. The authorities thought that because of the smallness of the parish it served, the church should be reconstructed in another part of the city where the need was greater.

An Act of Parliament was passed to obtain the necessary permission to close the church and move it. The last service in the church was held on 12 August 1877. Afterwards, the remarkable feat of taking it down stone by stone and numbering each one began. The stones were then taken a couple of miles across the city to Mina Road, where the new church was built, giving the area its name of St Werburghs. All the work was completed in just two years and the first service in the rebuilt church was held on 30 September 1879.

During the deconstruction, workmen found forty large chests of human remains and about 100 coffins, all of which were reinterred in Greenbank cemetery.

Sadly, St Werburgh's was made redundant as a place of worship just over 100 years later, due to a dwindling congregation. Since then the church, which was dedicated to a Saxon princess of the seventh century, has been put to another use as a rock climbing centre.

The original church site in Corn Street, along with its rectory, was acquired by a bank for just over £15,000. Its plans for a new building ran into trouble with the committee of the neighbouring Commercial Rooms, a coffee house where merchants and businessmen met to discuss issues of the day.

It was argued that the new bank would be built to such a height that it would obscure light from the reading room of the coffee house. The committee spent three years involved in litigation before finally succeeding in maintaining their rights.

⚜ CIVIC CUSTOMS ⚜

The title of Lord Mayor has a ring of antiquity about it, but in the context of Bristol's long and colourful history, it is relatively new.

In 1216 the office of mayor was created, with Roger Cordewaner having the privilege of being the first person to hold it. More than 600 years later, Herbert Ashman was the last mayor of Bristol. Twelve months later, in 1898, he was appointed the city's first Lord Mayor, a title which is the gift of the monarch of the day. Queen Victoria also decreed that the Lord Mayor could be addressed as the 'The Right Honourable'.

Shortly afterwards Mr Ashman was honoured with a knighthood. Usually, such an honour is conferred on the recipient at Buckingham Palace, but on this occasion Queen Victoria knighted Mr Ashman on the steps of the Council House, then in Corn Street. She didn't even leave her carriage to carry out the ceremony, instead merely leaning over and touching Mr Ashman, a leather merchant, on his shoulders with a borrowed sword.

Various royal charters have given the mayor some unusual rights. When John Noble was in office in 1762, he exercised his right to sit on the bench of any law court in the land. He did this on a visit to London, taking his seat in the Court of Admiralty, much to the surprise of the judge, who was already sitting there. Mr Noble was about to be ejected from the court when it was explained that he was privileged by an ancient charter to assert his right.

As His Lordship graciously offered the mayor a seat beside him, Noble rose, bowed and announced that having asserted the claim of his city, he would return home.

The mayoral year starts with a civic service in St Mark's chapel, opposite the council offices. It was founded in the thirteenth century as part of the Hospital of the Gaunts, which tended the sick, fed the poor and educated poor boys, although it could only accommodate twelve at any given time. The chapel was bought for £1,000 in 1541 by Bristol City Council, making it the only local authority in the country to own and maintain a place of worship. It is officially dedicated to St Mark but is better known as the Lord Mayor's chapel.

During his or her year of office, the Lord Mayor can expect to carry out approximately 1,000 engagements, ranging from opening church fetes to conferences, and from attending school prize-giving ceremonies to Christmas carol services.

In medieval days, one of the mayor's duties was to lead the annual tradition of Beating the Bounds. At this time, parish boundaries were marked by clergy and their congregations walking around them, striking a rod at certain points. As part of their ritual, the mayor and councillors were bumped on marker stones in an attempt to make them remember the boundary. They also took part in a duck hunt at Treen Mills, now known as Bathurst Basin. Unlike Beating the Bounds, it has not survived into the modern era; the last civic duck hunt took place in 1742.

As Bristol grew, taking in the villages around it, the land boundaries naturally expanded and in 1901, Beating the Bounds lasted two weeks. More than 200 councillors and civic officials took part.

Beating the Bounds was last attempted by Royston Griffey, during his tenure as Lord Mayor in 2007–08. While planning his journey on both land and water, Mr Griffey discovered that there are 47 square miles of Bristol underwater as opposed to 43 above.

Since 1373, when Bristol became a county, its water boundary has remained virtually unchanged. It extends to the Severn Estuary, to the islands of Steep Holm and Flat Holm, between Cardiff and Weston-super-Mare. The boundary also skirts around Clevedon Pier but includes the lighthouse at Battery Point, Portishead.

❖ COUNTING CHURCHGOERS ❖

The National Census introduced in England, Scotland and Wales in 1801 showed that the population of Bristol was then 66,000. Since then, a census has been conducted by the government every ten years. However, people living in the city in 1881 found themselves at the centre of an additional census: conducted by the *Western Daily Press*, this survey attempted to discover how many people went to church.

It was a most comprehensive census, for not only did it take in sixty-nine Anglican churches, but also those of other denominations, including Roman Catholic, Welsh Calvinistic, Methodist and Primitive Methodist. After the Church of England, the best attended places of worship were those of the Congregationalists, followed by the Salvation Army.

Statistics were supplied by the clergy and when the figures were analysed by the paper's editorial staff, they revealed that on the last Sunday in October, 45,518 people attended either a Church of England morning or evening service.

The newspaper reported that the largest congregation was at St Paul's church in the suburb of Southville, where 2,316 people attended the services. It was noted that the 'absence of the vicar would no doubt have caused the congregation to be less than usual'. A further 370 people turned up at the church's mission rooms in Ashton Gate and Albion Docks.

At the cathedral the clergy preached to 1,362 people at two services. Across the city at Old Market just under 1,300 people packed the pews for the services at St Philip and Jacob, trendily known today as Pip 'n' Jay. The census recorded that 'several people could not obtain admission to the evening service'.

The census showed that the church at Horfield Prison (now known as Her Majesty's Prison Bristol) had 147 worshippers, while the Red, White and Blue Temperance Army – with four meeting places across the city – counted a total of 523 churchgoers. At the Seamen's Christian Friend Society's floating chapel, the clergy preached to a total of 267 people at two services. The lowest attendance was said to be at the Swedenborgian church in Terrell Street, where just fifty-seven people were counted.

According to the *Western Daily Press*, a total of 109,452 people in Bristol went to church that Sunday. The paper estimated that a further 7,000 people living outside the city boundary had also gone to their local churches and chapels.

This was the first and so far only time that a count of churchgoers has been undertaken on this scale.

❧ CRICKET'S BIGGEST EVER SCORE ❧

It was on The Close that the world's biggest cricket score was made and has never been equalled or surpassed to this day by any club, county or international batsman. The player who went down in the record books was a 13-year-old pupil, Arthur Collins. He was at the crease for five afternoons in a junior house match in 1899 and scored 628 runs not out.

As he piled on run after run, people from all over the city made their way to the school to watch this remarkable young batsman. The cricket writers from the national press arrived in force too. *The Times* ran a simple headline: 'Collins Still In.' It was noted that in total he had stood before the wicket for nearly seven hours. The paper described Collins' score as 'astonishing' for his age.

Indeed, it was so unusual that it was recorded in *Wisden Cricketers' Almanack* – the cricketer's bible – and in the *Guinness Book of Records*. Two years later Collins knocked up a century for his school in a match against Old Cliftonians.

The Close at Clifton College (Trevor Naylor)

Not much seems to be known about his academic ability, but Collins was certainly a sporting all-rounder; besides cricket, Arthur especially enjoyed playing tennis for the school. With his formal education over, Collins went into the army at Woolwich Barracks, where he scored a century in a match against Sandhurst. He was also awarded a bronze medal for boxing.

Collins was commissioned into the Royal Engineers and after a posting in India, was sent to France with the British Expeditionary Force. Unfortunately, he was killed on the Western Front in the first year of the First World War.

His old college has never forgotten Collins' cricketing prowess. On the centenary of his big score, an anniversary match was staged with players wearing Victorian sporting kit. There is also a plaque at The Close commemorating him.

❧ *DEMERARA* DISASTER ❧

Many a fine ship has come to grief while making its way through the tortuous and twisting route of the Avon Gorge, either as it heads for the safe haven of the wharves in the city docks or leaves for the high seas.

In the sixteenth century the *Golden Lion* had safely made its way from Spain and across the Bay of Biscay when it ran into trouble in the mouth of the Bristol Avon. The ship missed the tide and, as she went into the Avon Gorge, toppled over. As the tide continued to fall, the *Golden Lion*, with its cargo of salt and fortified wine, sank.

But this was not the worst shipping disaster to occur: that happened in 1851, when the *Demerara* became stuck on her maiden voyage. She had been launched earlier in the year at Patterson's Shipyard at Wapping Wharf, and she was being towed by a powerful steam tug which had come down from Glasgow to take her to the Clyde for engines to be fitted.

The *Demerara* should have entered the River Avon some time before high water, so that the most dangerous part of the Avon Gorge could be passed with relative ease. But her tug set off too late. As the tide turned, the *Demerara*, with 1,200 tons of ballast, lurched out of control and struck the rocks of the Avon Gorge, just past the then unfinished Clifton Suspension Bridge.

She was refloated on the next tide, but once again broke away and became lodged across the river, blocking all navigation. The tug eventually pulled the ship back to the docks but she was so badly damaged that the assessor wrote her off. Large crowds gathered on the riverbank watching the rescue, part of which took place by torchlight.

But the builder of this wooden-hulled paddle steamship was undeterred. William Patterson, a canny Scot, ordered his workmen to remove the paddles so that the vessel could be repaired and converted into a passenger sailing ship. She was then renamed *British Empire*.

The *Demerara* had originally been built for the Royal West India Steam Packet Company, and was the second largest ship of her time at 3,000 tons. When Patterson retired to Liverpool, his son stayed in Bristol, specialising in – appropriately enough – marine salvage work.

A major feature of any sailing ship was its figurehead, which supposedly brought good luck, kept an eye on the crew and guided the vessel safely into harbour. A carving of a Red Indian was commissioned for the *Demerara*, which was proudly mounted beneath the bowsprit. For many years after the ship's disaster it was displayed on the front of an office in the city centre.

❧ THE DEMON BARBER ❧

Daredevil stunts were second nature to the man who earned the sobriquet 'the Demon Barber of Bedminster'.

There was no doubt about it – Charlie Stephens loved adventure and danger. He often shaved his customers in a lion's cage in the backyard of the old Red Cow Inn near his home. This attracted hundreds of people, who turned up to watch. In 1912 he carried out this particular stunt on the stage of the old Coliseum Theatre on Park Row.

Stephens, who was 58 years old, also offered himself as a target for knife throwers at the Victorian music halls, and even had an apple sliced in half on his throat with a sword. Wearing a distinctive red coat, he made parachute drops over his neighbourhood, once landing on a railway track just seconds before a train was due.

In 1920, Charlie Stephens organised a stunt to top all stunts. He planned to shoot himself over the Niagara Falls in a wooden barrel. No ordinary barrel, this; it was custom-built by a cooper, who usually made them for breweries.

Stephens had his 6ft-high barrel built from 2in-thick Russian oak. It was reinforced by a series of metal hoops and had a specially designed lid which could be released from the inside. Ballast was loaded into the bottom of the barrel, which Stephens thought would help to keep it upright in the water. It was also equipped with an oxygen tank and mask.

Ever the showman, he put the barrel on display at the Empire Theatre in Old Market before leaving for the Niagara Falls. Queues of people who wanted a close-up view were charged for a quick look. He also negotiated with a film company who wanted to film at the Niagara Falls. Undoubtedly, Stephens was trying to recoup some of his costs accrued in constructing the barrel.

Many friends tried to dissuade him from carrying out his madcap stunt, but all to no avail. Shortly after 8 a.m. on 11 July 1920, the barrel with Charlie inside was released into the river, about 2 miles above the Niagara Falls. Huge crowds had gathered to witness the event, but lost sight of the barrel halfway down its 160ft drop. Unfortunately, that was the last anyone saw of Charlie Stephens.

The next day some remains of one of his arms, bearing a tattoo expressing his love for his wife, Annie, were found in the water. Annie carried on Charlie's hairdressing business, without the stunts, putting one of her eleven children in charge.

❧ DOWNS SPORTS STARS ☙

Clifton and Durdham Downs, often referred to as the city's 'playground' or 'green lung', is home to one of the most unusual football leagues in the country. Every Saturday in the season, more than 500 men and youths turn up to play in the Downs League. More than fifty teams play in four divisions at the same time and on the same site.

Football matches on the Downs can be traced back to the 1880s, but it was not until 1905 that the fixtures became formalised and the Downs League was formed. Two clubs, St Andrews' and Sneyd Park, both taking their names from districts in the city, were among the league's founders and are still playing today.

The Downs League is a stand-alone league and does not feed into the English Football League system. However, some players have turned to greater things: Eddie Hapgood, who played for a club called Union Jack, went on to captain Arsenal and England in the 1930s. Other players signed professional papers for Bristol City, Bristol Rovers and West Bromwich Albion.

By all accounts, one of the most popular sporting activities on the Downs was horse racing. A two-day meeting was staged each May from around 1718 until 1838. According to one contemporary report, an 'immense number of spectators made their way to the makeshift course to place a bet'. It went on to say that 'the carriages were very numerous and filled with beautiful and elegant females which presented one of the most delightful scenes the imagination could portray.' The poet Alexander Pope referred to the 'fine turf' of the Downs and what he described as the 'delicious walking and riding'.

For the owners of winning horses there were various prizes, including velvet saddles, golden punchbowls and cash rewards, sometimes amounting to as much as 100 sovereigns.

Cricket, too, was popular, with Clifton Cricket Club playing on a pitch near the Sea Walls in 1819. On one occasion the chief constable reported an incident involving a lady crossing the pitch while play was in progress. What could arguably be called Gloucestershire's first county match took place on Durdham Down in July 1862. In a two-day game the Gentlemen of Gloucestershire defeated the Gentlemen of Devonshire by an innings and 77 runs.

❧ DOWRY SQUARE DISCOVERY ☙

If only walls could talk, the quiet backwater of Georgian houses in Dowry Square would have many a tale to relate. Thousands of motorists roar past the square on their way to work each day, probably unaware of its fascinating history. Few, if any, visitors stroll around Dowry Square, with its houses on three sides overlooking a central garden, open at the south end.

The square, built over thirty years from 1821 onwards, was developed to provide lodgings for visitors to the nearby Hotwells spa. In its early days, the square hosted some characters that have become the stuff of history books.

Part of its unusual background focuses on a three-storey L-shaped house that is tucked away in a corner and almost overshadowed by its next-door neighbour, a builder's office and yard.

It was at No. 6 that in 1797 a young Cornishman by the name of Humphry Davy knocked on the door to begin his scientific career. He had been offered the job of superintendent at Dr Thomas Beddoes' grandly named Pneumatic Institution.

The house where Humphry Davy worked (Janet Naylor)

Beddoes, who had been appointed reader of chemistry at Oxford University, was involved with controversial experiments to find a cure for such diseases as tuberculosis, asthma and dropsy. He came up with the idea that the gases produced by cows, at both ends, might be a cure for tuberculosis.

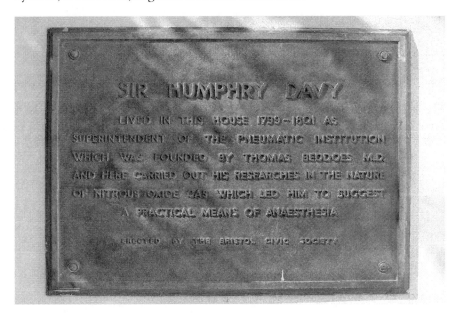

A plaque records the history of the Pneumatic Institution, Hotwells (Trevor Naylor)

He worked with Davy, investigating the medicinal effects of inhaling various gases. They were joined in their experiments by many of their friends from the literary set, including Romantic poets Samuel Taylor Coleridge and Robert Southey.

For some of his experiments, Dr Beddoes imported frogs from France. When hundreds of them escaped from their container while being unloaded at the docks, protestors marched on his home, although their reason for doing so is unknown.

In 1799 Davy discovered the anaesthetic properties of nitrous oxide, or laughing gas, a boon to dental patients (although not used for that purpose until much later), especially those undergoing extractions. Davy used nitrous oxide as both a painkiller and a recreational drug with his friends.

The Pneumatic Institution had a short life of about three years. Humphry Davy soon headed for London and the newly established Royal Institution where, at the age of 25, he was made Professor of Chemistry. He was knighted in 1812 by the Prince Regent for his contribution to science. Davy is probably best known for inventing the miner's safety lamp that now carries his name. Also working at the Pnuematic Institution as a physician and scientist was Peter Roget, who many years later published his famous thesaurus.

In the years after the Second World War Dowry Square became neglected and run-down, but it has now once again become a popular residential area.

ε

When William Bonny took advantage of the city fathers' lifting a by-law restricting trade to their own citizens, he started an industry which is still in existence.

Bonny was told that he could practice the trade of a printer, but would not be allowed to carry out any other business. He moved from London and set up a printing press, initially in Tower Lane where he mainly printed essays, before moving to nearby Small Street. It was there in 1702 that he founded and edited the city's first newspaper, *The Bristol Post-Boy*. It was also one of the first provincial papers in the country and is thought to have been published for about thirteen years. Coincidentally, in the twentieth century, his Small Street premises had become a public house and hotel, which was a popular haunt for newspaper journalists, along with barristers and judges who were working in the next-door law courts.

Bonny's paper was produced once a week as a single sheet, although it did not carry local news. Its strapline advertised the paper as 'giving an account of the most material news, both foreign and domestick'. Its content seems to have been garnered from London publications. The ninety-first issue of *The Bristol Post-Boy* is one of the earliest surviving copies of a provincial newspaper in the world; it is held by Bristol Reference Library.

Since Bonny's demise from the newspaper world dozens, if not scores, of would-be newspaper magnates have followed in his footsteps. Titles that have appeared over the last 300 years include *Felix Farley's Bristol Journal*, *Bristol Oracle*, *The Bristolian*, *Bristol Gazette*, *Bristol Mercury*, *Bristol Police Chronicle* and the *Clifton Chronicle*, to name just a few. Most of them were short-lived. However, the Farley family could be said to be the most successful by virtue of their longevity in the business. They started producing a newspaper in Exeter before moving to Bristol to publish *Sam. Farley's Bristol Post-Man* in 1713. Various branches of the family produced papers in the city for more than sixty years.

The late nineteenth century saw the birth of evening papers, and by 1920 Bristol had two, the *Evening News* and the *Evening Times and Echo*. Both publications faced fierce competition from a newcomer, the *Evening World*, part of a provincial chain run by the 1st Viscount Rothermere. Bristolians first had the chance of seeing his paper in 1929 when it rolled off the presses in a purpose-built newspaper office in Colston Avenue. The paper had a big promotions budget, designed to boost circulation quickly. Readers were offered, for example, a 5s book of National Savings Stamps if they signed up to buy the paper for ten weeks. By January 1932, both the *Bristol Evening News* and *Bristol Evening Times* had closed, leaving only the *Evening World*.

The paper faced strong opposition from Bristolians, though. They wanted a local paper run by local people. Sacked journalists and printers from the *News* and the *Times* joined a campaign led by the Bishop of Malmesbury to form a rival publication. They were joined by local businesses, with many individuals buying shares in the new venture. Enough money was soon raised to enable the first edition of the *Bristol Evening Post* to roll off the presses in a former leather factory in Silver Street on 18 April 1932. Reflecting its origins, every edition of the paper carries the legend, 'the paper all Bristol asked for and helped to create'.

Both papers continued to fight a tough circulation battle, which became known locally as 'the newspaper war'. It eventually became obvious, as it had in other cities, that it was no longer viable to publish two evening papers in Bristol. Sales of the *Evening World* had slumped from 80,000 copies to 30,000 a day and the last edition came off the presses at the end of January 1962. This left the *Post* as the only evening paper in the city, enjoying at the time a circulation in excess of 160,000 copies a day.

In an ironic move for the *Post*, almost forty years later Rothermere's Northcliffe group bought out its remaining independent shareholders. Yet another ownership change was to come at the start of 2012, however, when the *Post*, along with its stablemates, the *Western Daily Press* and the weekly *Observer* became part of a newly formed consortium, calling itself Local World. Today the papers are fighting another circulation battle, this time partly brought on by the advances of the internet providing an instant news source. Long gone are the days when paper sellers with their cries of 'Late Extra, Late Extra' were a familiar part of the street scene.

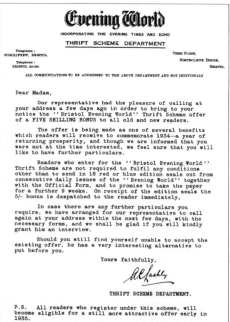

A letter sent to potential readers of Bristol's *Evening World* (Author's collection)

It's not generally known that Sir Tom Stoppard, the playwright and screenwriter, started his career as a journalist on the *Western Daily Press*. He worked on the paper from 1954–58, when he spent three years covering everything from court cases to championship matches at the Bristol Lawn Tennis Club. He then moved to the *Evening World* before leaving to concentrate on playwriting.

⚜ EXTRAORDINARY MEMORIALS ⚜

The churchyard of St Mary the Virgin at Henbury has two of the city's most intriguing graves. One of them features an Egyptian obelisk and a marble ankh, an object resembling a cross with a loop instead of the top arm. Ancient Egyptians regarded this as a symbol of life. Neither the obelisk nor the ankh is usually found at an Anglican place of worship.

The grave is the final resting place of Amelia Edwards, a Victorian journalist, novelist, traveller and Egyptologist, who spent the last thirty years of her life living in the neighbouring parish.

The grave of Amelia Edwards, with an obelisk and an ankh (Trevor Naylor)

Miss Edwards began her writing career when she was just 12 years old, with a short story that was published in a magazine. She went on to write numerous articles for newspapers and magazines, as well as writing several novels.

But a visit with friends to Cairo in 1873 changed her life forever. She became so outraged by the theft and vandalism of mummies, monuments and Egyptian artefacts that was going on that she made efforts to get it stopped. Back home in England, Edwards wrote a book entitled *A Thousand Miles up the Nile*, which was a serious study of the problem, intended to alert the public.

She founded the Egyptian Exploration Society, which

was designed to promote the excavation and proper care of artefacts. Running the organisation involved Edwards liaising with the Egyptian government to ensure that archaeological digs were carried out under stringent conditions. She insisted that detailed records be made about the discovery of artefacts and strategies which had been drawn up for their conservation.

Surprisingly, Amelia Edwards had no formal training as an archaeologist, but her own records and sketches of the ancient sites she found in Egypt have long been invaluable to academics. She is recognised as being one of the first archaeologists to encourage serious study of Egyptian antiquities. Her contribution to the field has been recognised by television documentaries and books about her life. She gave some of the

The ankh on the grave (Trevor Naylor)

treasures she rescued to Bristol Museum, while others were kept at her home at Westbury-on-Trym.

Whilst many of the tombstones in St Mary's churchyard are rather weather-beaten, making it almost impossible to read the epitaphs, another historic memorial has benefited from restoration. The head and footstones of the grave of Scipio Africanus are elaborately painted with black cherub faces.

The headstone simply states that Scipio was a 'Negro servant to the Right Honourable Charles William [Howard] … Earl of Suffolk and Bradon', who married Arabella Morse and lived at the Great House in Henbury. Charles was a wealthy and well-connected man who was a pageboy at the coronation of George I.

The date of Scipio's death is given on the tombstone as 21 December 1720, when he was just 18 years old. The footstone of his grave is inscribed with a verse which begins:

I, who was born a pagan and a slave,

Now sweetly sleep a Christian in my grave.

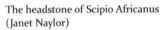

The headstone of Scipio Africanus
(Janet Naylor)

The footstone of Scipio Africanus
(Janet Naylor)

Little is known about the young man save that he came from West Africa and is believed to have been named after a Roman general. It's thought that he worked at the Great House for about five years. His employer and his wife both died in 1721 shortly after Scipio's death.

We shall never know how he arrived at Henbury, to be employed by one of the wealthiest families in the area. They must have thought a lot of him, for his grave is in a prominent position beside the footpath which leads to the church's main door. Scipio's tomb is one of the very few known memorials in this country to an African slave.

Churchyards are normally kept as the final resting places of former parishioners, but at St Mary Redcliffe church, one of the tombstones is simply engraved with the words 'Church Cat 1912–1927'. It marks the spot where the remains of Tom the tabby were buried. This feline was found at the priests' door to the south ambulatory of the church in 1912, attracted, some say, by the playing of the organ. He was befriended by the church staff and decided to stay.

Over the next fifteen years Tom became a popular member of the church community. According to records, he was fond of sitting by the side of the organist during part of the services. He was also adept at keeping down the number of pigeons that flocked to the churchyard and reported to be a good mouser.

Stephen Richards, grandson of Eli Richards, who was verger at the church between 1905 and 1925, once wrote that 'during the sermon Tom often used to sit on the lap of a member of the congregation'.

When Tom died, he was accorded what can only be described as a grand funeral for a four-legged creature. The organ was played as the vicar, verger, church wardens and several men from the choir processed into the churchyard. They sang a hymn as Tom's tiny coffin was lowered into his grave.

⚜ FEDDEN'S FORMIDABLE TASK ⚜

A new lease of life was given to the training ship *Formidable* when philanthropist and businessman Henry Fedden took her over from the Admiralty.

The ship was built in 1825 but never saw active service although for many years it was moored off Sheerness, Kent, as a flagship. When she was decommissioned, Henry Fedden, a sugar merchant in Bristol, had the ship brought around the south coast to Portishead, where she was anchored 400 yards off the pier for nearly forty years.

As chairman of Bristol's Board of Magistrates Henry Fedden was only too aware of the increasing number of boys and young lads wandering the streets homeless or appearing before the courts charged with truancy, theft or begging.

Fedden harboured a burning desire to inspire them to change their lifestyles so that they could become useful and lawful members of society. He converted the ship into a training school, which had room for up to 350 youngsters. This cost £3,000, with most of the money coming from fees that local people paid for trips to visit the ship. The school was officially opened in December 1869 by the Reverend Charles Kingsley, author of *The Water Babies* and *Westward Ho!*

Once on board, the boys were not only clothed and fed, but trained for service with either the Royal Navy or the Merchant Navy. Discipline and routine were strictly enforced; a typical day started with the boys swabbing the ship's decks. They started work at 5.30 a.m. in summer and an hour later in winter.

Henry Fedden ensured that academic studies played an important part in the youngsters' lives, with lessons on literacy and numeracy being given priority. Other subjects including cookery and carpentry were also taught.

Unfortunately, a number of deaths were recorded amongst the boys. Some were through the diseases of the time, although at least one lost his life through head injuries after falling out of his hammock and others fell overboard.

When the ship was considered beyond repair, largely because of its rotting hull, Fedden set about finding alternative premises on dry land. He leased a 15-acre plot of land nearby that was owned by Bristol Corporation and constructed a purpose-built stone school.

Fedden's project was regarded with much importance nationally and when the foundation stone of the new National Nautical School was laid, the ceremony was carried out by Queen Victoria's youngest daughter, Beatrice, Princess Henry of Battenburg. Her sister, Helena, Princess Christian of Schleswig-Holstein, was a guest of honour at the school's official opening in 1906. As part of the official proceedings, 350 boys marched to their new headquarters.

The school had links with the old ship, which had since been sold and taken to a breaker's yard. However, Henry Fedden ensured that its mizzenmast was given pride of place in the school's grounds. Some of the timbers from the *Formidable* were used in making the pulpit and lectern in the school's chapel, which was built on land in nearby Nore Road, freely given by Sir William Henry Wills of the famous Bristol tobacco family.

The National Nautical School closed in 1982, with the remaining pupils being transferred to another establishment in Bristol. The Grade II listed building was extended and renovated to become a gated development of apartments, maisonettes and houses, known as Fedden Village.

❧ FERRY AHOY! ❧

In a city with a river running right through it, separating the north from the south, ferries have long played a significant part in public transport. At one point, nine ferries crossed the River Avon at various points between Cumberland Basin and Temple Meads.

One of the earliest regular services owed its origins to the Abbot of St Augustine's abbey, which later evolved into Bristol Cathedral. He found the Rownham Ferry a quick and convenient way of getting to his home in the country, at Abbots Leigh. It was privately run, but later passed into the ownership of the church authorities, finally being bought by Bristol Corporation for £10,000. The ferry last sailed in 1932.

The Mardyke Ferry, further along the floating harbour towards the city centre, was one of the busiest water crossings. It carried workers from Hotwells to the Charles Hill Albion shipyard on the other side of the harbour. Early in the reign of Queen Victoria, it carried men who were working on Brunel's SS *Great Western* and the SS *Great Britain* at Patterson's shipyard. Later, it ferried women and girls to work in the Wills tobacco factories at Bedminster and Ashton.

In the 1960s, more than a century after the Mardyke Ferry made its first crossing, the Port of Bristol Authority brought down the economic axe, claiming it was losing £900 a year. Regular passengers organised petitions objecting to the proposed closure, but it still went ahead. The ferry is remembered in the name of a pub close to its old slipway.

Some ferries were set up by local industrialists. John Acraman, the owner of an iron foundry who also had interests in ship building, started the Gaol Ferry. It provided a link across the River Avon, or New Cut, between people in Southville and the city centre. Acraman's ferry service began in 1828 and in its first twenty-five years carried approximately 1 million passengers, who paid a penny each to cross the River Avon. The ferry went out of business in 1935, when Bristol Corporation built a bridge across the river just yards from the slipway, which can still be seen.

The ferry which linked the village of Shirehampton with the village of Pill on the Somerset side of the river was also put out of business by a new bridge. For many years a rowing boat carried commuters across the river, but in the twentieth century it was replaced by a motorboat. In the 1950s the ferry service was owned by a tugboat firm, who leased it to a family in Pill. There were so many passengers that three boats were crossing the river from 5 a.m. to nearly 11 p.m. Great skill was needed by the ferrymen in crossing the Avon, as at this point it runs rather swiftly.

When the M5 road bridge opened, several miles downstream at Avonmouth, it was inevitable that the number of ferry passengers would dwindle. Pill ferry therefore made its last crossing at the end of 1974.

But the oldest ferry of them all is probably the one that ran across the River Severn from Aust on the Gloucestershire bank to Beachley, near Chepstow. It is known that the Romans ferried their legions across the estuary on galleys at this point. In more recent times, the ferry carried cars and motorcycles as well as foot passengers. Trade was always brisk, as motorists from Bristol and the West Country saw it as a quick cut to Wales, avoiding a much longer journey by road via Gloucester. But when the first Severn Bridge opened in 1966, linking England with Wales, the Aust Ferry sadly closed.

THE FLOATING HARBOUR CREATED

What must have been an unprecedented piece of engineering work for the time started at the beginning of May 1804, when the first sods of earth were dug to create the floating harbour.

This involved impounding 80 acres of the tidal River Avon, to enable ships to stay afloat constantly while they were in the docks, either loading or discharging their cargoes. Normally, ships would become stranded in the mud of the docks after the tide receded. At low tide, all ships in the port would run aground. A floating harbour, though, would mean that the water level in the docks was always constant.

The dock authorities decided that such a scheme was essential if the port was to expand, take bigger ships and provide a quicker turnaround for cargo handling (the city's prosperity was being threatened as traders began to choose other ports so that they could avoid the tides in the harbour).

The man commissioned to build the floating harbour was William Jessop, who had started work on canal construction when he was just 16 years old. His work all over the country had established him as one of the country's leading civil engineers. Jessop employed his son to supervise the project, which involved obtaining an Act of Parliament to divert a 2-mile-long stretch of the River Avon from Cumberland Basin to Totterdown. The estimated cost of the project, including the land, was £300,000, but in the event the bill came to double that.

Approximately 1,000 men were employed on digging and blasting what has since become known as the New Cut. The tools they used were mainly shovels, picks and wheelbarrows. Gunpowder was used to blast through the rock. Much of the hard sandstone was later used to build the walls of the locks that were needed at Cumberland Basin, and the water basins that had to be created as a result.

Five years to the day after work started on digging the New Cut, Jessop's scheme was completed. The new waterway was also used for navigation, with early passenger steam packets sailing to South Wales and Ireland from a jetty that had been built at the Bathurst Basin.

To celebrate the creation of the floating harbour, an open-air party was laid on for the 1,000 men who had been working on it. They were treated to a menu of roast oxen, potatoes, plum pudding and a gallon of beer each. Perhaps unsurprisingly, with the amount of alcohol being consumed, a brawl broke out between the English and Irish workmen.

Bristol City Council closed the harbour to commercial shipping in 1975 for economic reasons. The docklands area has since been regenerated beyond all recognition with old rotting and rusting cargo sheds and derelict railway sidings being replaced with offices, hundreds of apartments, restaurants and cafes. The water itself has also become a leisure and recreation area. It is home to such events as the annual Harbour Festival, attracting hundreds of pleasure craft, tall ships and naval vessels. Many people have also taken to living on the water in houseboats. Water taxis glide around the harbour ferrying commuters to work, too.

⚘ FLOWER OF BRISTOL ⚘

Many countries have floral emblems as a national symbol. Canada, for example, is associated with the maple leaf, while nearer home, Ireland is linked with the shamrock, Scotland with the thistle, and Wales with the leek. There can't be many cities or towns, though, which have their own flower, but Bristol has the Flower of Bristowe (an ancient spelling of the city's name).

The earliest reference to the plant in this country is found in Gerard's *Herball, or General Historie of Plantes* of 1633 in which it is described as the 'Floure of Bristowe or None-such … that is a torch of such like light, cleere, bright and light giving'.

The Flower of Bristowe comes from eastern Russia. Its seeds were believed to have been taken to Mediterranean countries, where it became known by various names, including the Maltese Cross. Seafaring traders are thought to have brought the flower to Bristol.

Its local name derives from the similarity of the flower's colour to a bright red dye made in the sixteenth century, known as 'Bristowe Red'. It seems to have been a popular colour in those days. The merchant John Whitson, who bequeathed money to set up the Red Maids' School, left instructions in his will that the girls should be 'apparelled in red cloth'. Red uniform is still worn by the girls and the colour can also be seen on the city's heraldic shield.

With the passage of time, the Flower of Bristowe has become the city's unofficial floral emblem. It grows wild in parts of the Avon Gorge but can be seen in the gardens of West Mall in the heart of Clifton Village, alongside a descriptive plaque. The plant grows to around 2–3ft high, and each summer it produces small five-petalled florets, shaped like a cross.

This is not the only plant to be associated with Bristol, though. The Avon Gorge is home to around thirty different rare and uncommon plants. One of them, the Western Spiked Speedwell, with its purple-blue flowers, grows on the steep limestone cliffs of St Vincent's Rocks, near the Clifton Suspension Bridge. It was first recorded in Britain in the Avon Gorge in 1634.

Another native is the Bristol Onion, also known as the round-headed leek. It only grows naturally in this country in the gorge, and it was discovered in 1847. The many crevices of the gorge are the only places in the United Kingdom where the Bristol Rock Cress grows wild.

Nine wild plants with an important historical and conservation association with Bristol have been planted in a flowerbed specially built at the Clifton entrance of the Clifton Suspension Bridge. It's an appropriate spot, for when work started on the bridge, its designer was alerted that rare plants were at risk of being destroyed by construction work. Isambard Brunel therefore had them carefully dug up and replanted elsewhere in the gorge.

⚜ GOLDNEY'S GROTTO ⚜

Screened from passing eyes by a high forbidding grey stone wall is the only grotto in Britain with a shell room and running water.

Goldney Grotto, not particularly well known, was designed by Thomas Goldney as the centrepiece of the 12-acre garden at his palatial mansion high up on Clifton Hill, overlooking the city. His grotto, approached through a long tunnel, is covered with more than 200 types of exotic seashells, tiles, pieces of quartz, coral, rocks and fossils.

Goldney, an eighteenth-century merchant, who was a director of Goldney, Smith & Co. – the second bank to open in Bristol – had ordered his captains to bring back the shells from their overseas privateering expeditions. They were found at exotic locations in the South Seas and the Caribbean; on beaches and prised from cliffs and caves. From much nearer home Goldney included the so-called Bristol Diamonds – red- and coral-coloured minerals excavated from the cliffs of the Avon Gorge near Clifton Suspension Bridge.

Goldney started work on his 36ft-long grotto in 1737. It took him nearly thirty years to cover all its corners and crevices, as well as including a fountain and several statues. It is now a Grade I listed building.

Goldney's taste for the finer things in life didn't stop at creating a grotto. He covered the walls of the dining room in his mansion with mahogany, at the time a new wood, which had been brought back from the West Indies.

After the last of the Goldney family died, the house and its grounds passed into various hands. At one time it was owned by Lewis Fry of the chocolate family and later by Sir George Wills, the tobacco baron. In 1956 the house and grounds were bought by the University of Bristol, and it is now a student hall of residence known as Goldney Hall. The grotto is only open on certain days of the year.

⚜ THE GUNPOWDER HOUSE ⚜

The Powder House certainly lived up to its name in the past. It was here that ships' captains, making their way up the River Avon into Bristol, had to unload any barrels of gunpowder or any other inflammable material they had on board. They could reclaim it on their way out of Bristol back into the Severn Estuary.

With the masts of so many wooden ships almost touching each other in the wharves at Hotwells it's easy to see why the port authorities were being cautious about preventing any possible explosion or fire. Indeed, in 1776 they obtained an Act of Parliament in order to 'remove the danger of fire amongst the ships in the port of Bristol by preventing the landing of certain commodities on the present quays, and for providing a convenient quay and proper places for landing and storing the same'.

That 'convenient quay' was the specially built Powder House, on the north bank of the River Avon, almost overhanging the treacherous Horseshoe Bend. It was built at about the same time as the Act of Parliament was passed.

The Powder House consisted of two buildings. One was equipped with a crane for lifting the barrels of gunpowder and the other building was the storeroom. It's believed the premises were last used for this purpose towards the end of the nineteenth century.

The Powder House is still there but has been sensitively converted into a private residence.

⟩⟨ HIGH CROSS ⟩⟨

Passed by hundreds of office workers every day, but rarely given a glance, are the remains of a replica of the Bristol High Cross. The original stood for more than 500 years at the junction of High Street, Wine Street, Corn Street and Broad Street, the ancient heart of the old city. By all accounts it was rather grand, standing about 40ft high, brightly painted and gilded and with statues of medieval kings who had granted charters to the city in its niches.

The remains of the replica of the Bristol High Cross stand in Berkeley Square, Clifton. The original is in the grounds of Stourhead Park, Wiltshire (Trevor Naylor)

Indeed, the cross itself marked the granting of a charter by Edward III in 1373 which made Bristol a county in its own right, separating it from the adjoining counties of Somerset to the south and Gloucestershire to the north and granting the city its own sheriff. The charter was a reward for Bristol's patriotism in supplying twenty-two ships and 662 mariners to the king at the Siege of Calais. This was only three ships and fifty-four men less than London sent.

The High Cross was not only a landmark; it became the location for civic proclamations and a place where councillors assembled for processions.

Sometime in the seventeenth century it was moved after people living nearby complained that it was a 'ruinous and superstitious relick which presents a public nuisance on account of its hazardous condition'. The monument was removed to

College Green, the triangular piece of land in front of City Hall, which is leased to the council by the Dean and Chapter of Bristol Cathedral. But even here it attracted complaints, from those who claimed it was obstructing a footpath. The cross was eventually taken down and stored in bits in a cloister of the cathedral.

And that was the last the city saw of its High Cross, for the Dean of Bristol, Dr Cutts Barton, eventually gave it to his friend Henry Hoare II, who installed it on his estate at Stourhead Park, Wiltshire. It has stood there since 1768 and is now maintained by the National Trust, which owns the park.

A replica of the cross was commissioned and again stood on College Green until 1950, when the land was lowered. The replica found its way into a builder's yard, where it was left to

A detail from the Bristol High Cross (Trevor Naylor)

crumble. An appeal was set up by conservation groups to restore the replica, and today the top part of it stands in a corner of a communal garden in Berkeley Square, Clifton.

❖ HOGARTH'S 'SECRET' PAINTING ❖

It could be called Bristol's secret painting, for few people are aware that a Hogarth masterpiece has a home in the city. The painting is so big – 800 sq ft to be exact – that it stands on a stage and looks down on office workers, their desks, computers, and filing cabinets. And those who know of the painting have to make private arrangements to view it.

The story of this painting started in 1755, when the church wardens at St Mary Redcliffe commissioned William Hogarth – artist, satirist, engraver and social critic – to paint an altarpiece for their church. He produced three huge canvases, known as a triptych, which he called *Sealing the Tomb*. Each canvas depicted a different scriptural scene: 'The Ascension', 'Sealing of the Sepulchre' and 'The Three Marys at the Tomb', respectively. Hogarth took a year to complete the commission, for which he was paid £525. A Bristol architect, Thomas Paty, was engaged to design and make gilded frames for each of the canvases.

When the paintings arrived at St Mary Redcliffe, however, they turned out to be too wide for the allotted space. The centre piece measured 22ft by 19ft, while the side panels were each 13ft 10in by 12ft. This meant that the side panels had to stand at an angle.

One hundred years later, the church authorities decided that the triptych was no longer suitable for St Mary Redcliffe. They decided to sell it, contacting the National Gallery and Christie's Auction Rooms in London and advertising it in *The Times*, but without any success.

The paintings then began a somewhat nomadic life. In 1859 they were given to the Bristol Fine Art Academy, later to be known as the Royal West of England Academy of Art. Another attempt to find a buyer was made in 1910, but in vain. The canvases were eventually rolled up and put into storage. They spent the Second World War in the basement of Bristol Museum and Art Gallery.

In 1955 they were officially acquired by the gallery, with help from the National Arts Collection Fund. Towards the end of the twentieth century, the triptych was taken to St Nicholas' church, overlooking Bristol Bridge. The inside of the church was destroyed in Bristol Blitz. However, during restoration, an upper storey was formed, which became an ecclesiastical museum.

This provided an ideal showcase for Hogarth's work, along with ecclesiastical artefacts from other churches in the Diocese of Bristol. However, the museum closed in 2007. Since then it has been an office for city council staff. The triptych is still there and can be seen by members of the public, but only by appointment during office hours.

❧ HORSE-DRAWN TRAMS ROW ❧

It's hard to believe that controversy surrounded the introduction of such a leisurely form of travel as horse-drawn trams.

In the 1870s, though, Bristol Corporation decided to build a tramway and set up Bristol Tramways Company to run it. Their plans immediately ran into fierce opposition from people living in Clifton, who feared that 'hordes of working class people would arrive in the sedate suburb'.

Churchgoers joined the argument, claiming that the trams would encourage workers to seek out 'sinful pleasures'. The writer of a letter which was published in the *Bristol Mercury* asked: 'Is it not something terrible and most wicked that the disgusting tramway is to bring the nasty low inhabitants of Bristol up to our sacred region?' Shopkeepers also voiced their concern, pointing out that trams would enable people to shop in the centre of the city, rather than spend their money with the shopkeepers of Clifton.

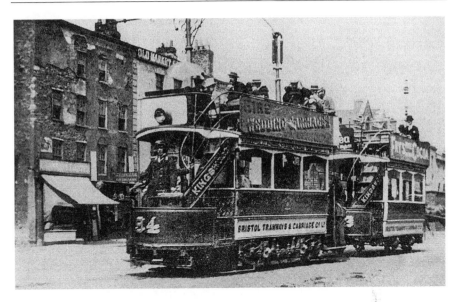

A tram on the Old Market to Kingswood service (Author's collection)

The tramway bosses went ahead with the scheme, however, and the first horse-drawn tram in the city went into service in 1875. It ran from a depot (now a microbrewery), in Perry Road to St John's church on Whiteladies Road. The service was so popular that 115,000 passengers used the tram in its first month. Eventually horse-drawn trams were operating on ten routes in the city.

Electric trams started twenty years later, and at its peak, services ran on seventeen routes with a total of 237 cars. Bristol was one of the first cities to adopt electric trams and by 1908, the network of 31 miles running around the city and into south Gloucestershire was complete. When the first one ran from Old Market to Kingswood, to the east of the city, many offices and factories closed so their workers could witness the historic occasion.

In 1937, Bristol Corporation took up its option to buy the tramway company, for which it paid £1.25 million. It also promised to replace the trams with motor buses. A few trams were still running at the outbreak of the Second World War, but the service they provided came to an abrupt end when a bomb fell near the generating station, cutting their power supply. All of the city's trams were then scrapped.

⚜ THE HOTEL BUILT BY BRUNEL ⚜

It's well known that Isambard Kingdom Brunel built bridges, railways, ships and even hospitals for overseas countries, but it's not generally known that he was also involved with a hotel.

Brunel was someone who obviously didn't do things by halves, for he saw the Royal Western Hotel as an integral part of the journey from London to New York.

Passengers would board their train at Paddington and travel to Bristol on the railway that Brunel had built, spending the night at his elegant hotel before boarding the SS *Great Western*, his transatlantic steamer.

Brunel worked with a Bristol architect, Richard Shackleton, to build the two-storey hotel of Bath stone with a classical façade of Corinthian pillars. For the comfort of guests, especially during inclement weather, their coaches could approach the hotel through an arched entrance to a covered yard, where up to fifty horses could be stabled.

The Royal Western Hotel was opened in 1838 amidst much pomp and ceremony, with the Lord Mayor being guest of honour at an inaugural banquet. Unfortunately, Bristol's bid for the transatlantic trade was a flop. The SS *Great Western* was forced by the Cunard shipping company to make Liverpool her port of call. It meant that just a few years after opening, Brunel's hotel had closed and become a Turkish bath.

It remained a hydro-cooling room and cold plunge for many years. Doctor Arthur Spoor, who ran it, was a keen gardener and turned the high area at the back of an amphitheatre adjoining the hotel into a hanging garden. This amphitheatre was home to a horse bazaar, where horses and carriages were bought and sold. No doubt some horses would have been bought to pull the city's horse-drawn buses. There was also a room for a coach maker.

Brunel's Royal Western Hotel is now council offices (Trevor Naylor)

Statues that recall the days of horse trading on this spot (Trevor Naylor)

The hotel building in St George's Road still stands, although it was threatened with demolition in the 1960s (despite the old Ministry of Housing describing it as 'one of the finest monumental buildings in the West of England'). It was placed on the government's Grade II list of buildings of architectural merit. That move thwarted plans for the hotel to be replaced by a nine-storey office block. Instead the building was given a facelift, which retained its splendid exterior. It is now used as overspill offices for council workers from City Hall on the opposite side of the road.

As a tribute to the great engineer, the building has been named Brunel House. In another nod to history a tiny plaque recording the building's original use – so small that it is unnoticed by thousands of passers-by – is fixed to a side wall.

The amphitheatre, unknown to many, is still there. A bronze statue of a man and a horse recalling an episode from its colourful past stands in the middle, although much of the space has been given over to car park spaces.

⚜ INVENTORS GALORE ⚜

Bristol has had more than its fair share of inventors and pioneering industrialists. Some of them came up with weird and whacky ideas for changing the world, while others were just simply ahead of their time.

William Champion pioneered the working of brass and zinc at his eighteenth-century works at Warmley on the edge of the city; Abraham Darby perfected the casting of ironware at a brass foundry in Baptist Mills and Joseph Fry produced chocolate which he made famous all over the world.

It wasn't just men who were taking out patents to protect their ideas. Sarah Guppy of Clifton had spent a lifetime designing gadgets and machines. She took out her last patent when she was aged 74. Amongst her ideas was a method for keeping ships free of barnacles, a four-poster bed with built-in exercise equipment, and a multi-purpose tea and coffee urn that could cook eggs and keep toast warm.

Perhaps one of the most eccentric inventors, though, was George Pocock, a man of many parts. He was a travelling evangelistic preacher, a church organist and a leading exponent of what he called the new science of aeropleustics. All this, as well as running his own school.

Pocock put his inventive mind to use at his school in Prospect Place, off St Michael's Hill. As a visual aid for his pupils' geography lessons, he designed an inflatable globe of the world. There was also a mechanical device he called a 'thrashing machine' for punishing errant pupils. It consisted of a rotating wheel with artificial hands which whacked an offending schoolboy without any human effort involved.

But it was his invention of an open horseless carriage that generated headlines, not only in Britain's weekly papers, but in the American press too. Pocock discovered that large kites, flown on long lines, provided enough power to propel vehicles on land and sea. He called his four-wheeled carriage a 'Charvolant' and found that it could reach speeds that out-distanced horse-drawn carriages. Handling the tiller was an art in itself, for the driver had to prevent kites becoming entangled in trees. Pocock fastened the tiller to the front wheels by means of a vertical shaft. In the Charvolant's early days he took a spare horse with him, in case he and his passengers were becalmed. The horse was carried on a wheeled platform behind the carriage.

Much to the bemusement of his pupils, George Pocock used members of his family as guinea pigs to demonstrate his new form of transport, which he patented in 1826. His wife and children were taken on journeys around the country, including trips to London and Marlborough and across Salisbury Plain. Bristolians flocked to the Durdham Down Races in 1828 when Pocock gave a demonstration of the Charvolant in action. After that he was invited to take it to a race meeting at Ascot, which was attended by George VI. However, Pocock's invention never got off the ground, although it could not have been for the lack of trying on his part.

Pocock also tried to interest the army in using kite-powered convoys, guided by aerial spotters, but to no avail. There was no interest either from the navy in his life-saving devices. Pocock even demonstrated with his daughter Martha how survivors from shipwrecks could be carried in baskets powered by kites on to cliffs and beaches. He also took a three-week long cruise in the Bristol Channel, in a yacht, to test the effect of replacing the sails with kites.

Pocock, in an effort at demonstration, made a 30ft kite to lift 15-year-old Martha, strapped into a kitchen chair, high above the Avon Gorge. Fortunately, the girl was none the worse for her adventure as she went on to marry Henry Mills Grace. Their five sons included Dr W.G. Grace, the Gloucestershire cricketing legend.

Pocock went on write a 'Treatise on the Aeropluestic Art or Navigation in the Air'. He never missed an opportunity to promote his interests. When the Clifton Suspension Bridge foundation stone was laid on the Somerset side of the Avon Gorge, he turned up with his pupils. They released into the air five balloons between 12 and 20ft in circumference. Attached to one of them was a streamer inscribed with the words 'Success to the undertaking'.

$\mathcal{J}$

⁂ JACOB'S WELL SET FOR REVIVAL ⁂

For a medieval relic, believed to be unique in this country and possibly Europe, the building at the junction of Constitution Hill and Jacob's Wells Road has been put to a strange variety of uses.

It was once a bicycle shed for constables at the police station that stood on the beauty spot of Brandon Hill on the opposite side of the road. It has also been a workshop for the restoration of antiques and at one time was part of the local fire station. Yet behind its high curving stone wall, out of sight and possibly not given a thought by the thousands of commuters that pass it every day, is a well and a sacred stone bathing place. It is listed by the government as a scheduled ancient monument, thought to date back to about 1140.

Jacob's Well is housed in this building (Trevor Naylor)

Jacob's Well, as it is called, was used in Jewish burial ceremonies where the bodies of the deceased were washed before internment. The water had to be untouched by man, either derived from a natural spring or from rainwater. A lintel inside the building bears an inscription in Hebrew, only partly visible now, which presumably means 'living water'.

There was a Jewish settlement at Hotwells as Jews were banned from living inside the city itself. The site for their ritual bath was probably chosen because of its closeness to a Jewish burial ground. Known as Jews' Acre, the cemetery now lies underneath Queen Elizabeth Hospital, built on the slopes of Brandon Hill in 1847 when the school moved from the centre of the city. Gravestones found at the time are believed to have been used in building the school. This was the first Jewish cemetery in Bristol, established in the medieval period.

Like Jews down the ages, they suffered much persecution; a man who refused to pay heavy ransom money to King John was taken off to Bristol Castle. One of his teeth was pulled out each day by the king's torturers. Seven teeth were extracted before he paid up.

There was wholesale expulsion of the Jews from England in 1290. Under the Edict of Expulsion, Jews were forbidden from destroying religious artefacts, even if they were no longer used. This led to many of their sacred sites becoming lost or forgotten.

After the banishment of the Jews, the spring that feeds Jacob's Well passed to the Crown, who allowed the monks of St Augustine's Abbey to use it. When King Edward III granted Bristol the right to become a county in 1373, he also gave the spring to the city. Down the years it has had various owners. In 1840 a private company bottled and sold the water, describing it as 'Genuine Superior Aerated Waters'.

After its many and varied uses, commercialism could now be back at Jacob's Well. A newly formed company that has taken ownership has been given permission by the Environment Agency to extract and bottle up to 3.3 million gallons of water a year.

English Heritage apparently regards Jacob's Well as potentially a monument of the highest importance, both for the history of the Jewish community in England and for medieval studies in general. Furthermore, the site is potentially of international importance.

K

✥ KILN BECOMES A RESTAURANT ✥

These days the Redcliffe and Temple districts are a world away from the seventeenth-century skyline dotted with the cones of glass-making kilns belching out clouds of black smoke.

The glass-making industry didn't go unnoticed either by the poet Alexander Pope who visited the spa at Hotwells in 1739. He described the kilns as 'twenty odd pyramids smoking over the town'. In their place now are numerous developments of flats huddling close to the nondescript office blocks of glass and steel. But one cone, or to be precise, the lower part of it, still stands. It is part of the last working kiln at Redcliffe, which closed in 1923.

The cone was originally 60ft high, but the top of it was taken down in 1936 for safety reasons. Thirty years later, officers from Bristol City Council toyed with the idea of turning this remnant of an historic industry into a museum of glass and glass technology. In the event, though, it was incorporated into a new hotel as a restaurant.

The base of the last kiln in Bristol used for making glass has been incorporated into a hotel as a restaurant (Trevor Naylor)

This part of Bristol was particularly suited to the glassmaking industry due to its proximity to Redcliffe Caves and the docks. These man-made caves of red sandstone were excavated between the fifteenth and seventeenth centuries providing the huge quantities of sand that was needed in glass-making. Glassmakers were then able to easily export their products – ranging from window glass to bottle glass – through the nearby city docks.

Bristol was one of the most important glass-making centres in Europe. Its world-famous Bristol Blue Glass was first made in the seventeenth century, but as the trade declined the kilns, which were something of a landmark, disappeared.

The Kiln Restaurant stands on the site of another bit of the city's industrial history: the track of the old Bristol Harbour railway. It ran above ground from Temple Meads station, across the hotel site and then under St Mary Redcliffe churchyard, to emerge from a tunnel at Bathurst Basin.

❧ KING'S SHOPPING MALL ❧

It may surprise many people to learn that the city's first indoor shopping centre was built more than a century ago. It was the brainchild of Joseph King, a self-taught

Clifton arcade, with its rose window (Janet Naylor)

architect, builder and entrepreneur. He had already built a row of shops on Whiteladies Road and a small terrace of houses in Clifton, but his Royal Bazaar and Winter Gardens was something much grander.

It was a most ambitious scheme, involving two buildings as well as gardens. There was not only the shopping arcade itself; at right angles to it stood a reception and entrance way with enough space for carriages to drive inside.

The two floors of shops in the arcade in Boyce's Avenue, Clifton, were linked with a grand sweeping staircase, graced by two neoclassical columns. Joseph King thought of every comfort for his potential shoppers, including the provision of a glass roof to protect them from inclement weather. Also provided were '[a] grand restaurant, private dining rooms, and toilets'. Live music was planned for six hours every Saturday, although the arcade would be open for twelve hours every day. After their shopping experience, customers could relax among the trees and shrubs in the Winter Gardens that King had built on 20,000ft of space on what is now Clifton Down Road. The arcade cost King £10,500, and he hoped to recoup this from the retail units he would rent out to individual traders. King himself would be the general manager.

A day of festivities was arranged for the opening of the arcade in the spring of 1878, with a 'celebratory band' providing musical accompaniment. But it all turned out to be a flop. None of the trading spaces had been let, leaving the arcade empty. It soon became known as King's Folly. The entrepreneur went bust and three months later, the arcade was offered for sale by auction. By the end of the year, the building was occupied by the Wilsonia Depot, which specialised in magnetic belts, corsets and vests. But this business was doomed, too.

For the next 100 years, King's arcade was used as a warehouse by the Knee Brothers, who ran a furniture storage business. When Edward Knee died in 1985, the building was left to fall into disrepair. However, in the 1990s, a firm of developers restored the arcade and filled the units with independent traders, which survive to this day.

❖ LAW AND ORDER ❖

From the Middle Ages onwards, those who broke the law were often punished by having to spend time in the stocks, where they could be pelted with bad fruit. Almost every parish had its own pair of stocks. It is recorded that in 1826, two men were ordered to spend three hours each in the stocks on Redcliffe Hill after being found in a drunken state in a churchyard.

Wives who nagged could be punished with a session in the ducking stool. Women were strapped into this contraption and dipped in the River Frome three times. The city beadles received a payment of 2s for each woman they ducked. Meanwhile, bakers who sold underweight bread were put in a cage in Wine Street, near the High Cross.

A charter granted to Bristol by Edward III also provided the city with a gaol, so that offenders could be deprived of their liberty. For many years, the gaol was at Newgate (the Galleries shopping centre now stands on the site). Those languishing inside had to rely on the generosity of local people for food, because no meals were provided by the prison authorities. Newgate Prison was replaced in 1821 by the New Gaol on Cumberland Road, which was built with a trapdoor on its roof for public hangings. It is unthinkable these days, but hangings were treated as major events which became favourite outings for many a family.

The New Gaol's first hanging took place nine months after it had opened. Thousands of people gathered outside to watch the last moments of John Horwood, who had an appointment with the hangman just three days after his eighteenth birthday. So many people were standing along the unfenced New Cut, or River Avon, that notices had to be displayed warning them about the danger of falling into the water. The huge crowd of people saw Horwood stand for twenty-five minutes on the gaol's rooftop platform before summoning enough courage to indicate to the hangman that he was ready to meet his maker by dropping his handkerchief. Horwood had been convicted of killing his sweetheart. It was said in court that during a lover's tiff, he threw a stone, or pebble at her, a distance of 30 yards. It caught the girl on her head and she died in hospital three weeks later.

The remains of the gaol on Cumberland Road (Author's collection)

A remarkable 50,000 people are said to have jostled each other trying to find the best vantage point when Mary Ann Burdock was hanged for murder sixteen years later. She had been convicted of murdering an elderly lodger by poisoning her so that she could get hold of her savings. Silence fell on the crowd when two figures appeared on the scaffold, which had been erected overnight. Their job was to lead Burdock to the hangman.

In 1849, Sarah Ann Thomas was the last person to be hanged at the New Gaol. The 17-year-old servant girl had been found guilty of killing her elderly employer, Miss Elizabeth Jefferies; she had bludgeoned her to death with a stone while she was sleeping. Thomas had claimed that she was a hard taskmaster.

Throughout her trial at the Assize Courts Thomas had not appeared to treat the proceedings seriously. However, records show that when the judge donned his black cap to pass the death sentence she collapsed and completely broke down. Thomas continued to sob, scream and plead for her life right up until the final moment. The newspapers reported that so 'great and moving was the awful scene' that even the prison governor fainted, he was so overcome.

In 1831, when Bristol witnessed some of the worst civil disturbances in its history, the gaol was attacked by rioters. They had broken away from a much larger crowd in nearby Queen Square which was protesting about the Reform Bill, then being debated in parliament.

Rioters breached the prison's iron gates after battering them with sledgehammers, hatchets and crowbars. A small boy was able to get inside the gates and draw back the bolts. The inevitable happened and nearly 200 prisoners were freed, joining the mob. They set fire to the treadmill and gallows, along with the governor's house and the prison chapel. Order was eventually restored by troops called in from Gloucester, who fired on the crowd, killing more than 100 people.

The prison closed in 1883, when the government condemned it as inadequate. It was replaced by the present gaol at Horfield. Bristol Corporation bought the land for the gaol from the Bristol Pleasure Garden Company for £3,875.

Although hangings continued to take place, they were no longer in public. The last hanging at Horfield Prison took place on 17 December 1963 at the traditional time of 8 a.m. Russell Pascoe, aged 24, went to the gallows for his part in the murder of a 64-year-old recluse living in a remote Cornish farmhouse. Protestors, including the Bishop of Bristol, who were objecting to the death sentence, staged a vigil outside the prison's main gates. The Rt Revd Oliver Tomkins asked his fellow protestors to spare a thought for the executioners who 'have to do this awful job'. Two years later, parliament abolished the death penalty for murder and in its place imposed a sentence of mandatory life imprisonment.

Meanwhile, the crumbling gateway of the New Gaol, with its grey side towers of granite, is all that remains of that building. English Heritage has put these ruins on the Grade II list of buildings of architectural or historical interest.

The gateway is to be refurbished as the centrepiece of a new pedestrian route into a multi-million pound housing development to be built around it. It will be a permanent reminder to Bristolians of a grim part of their city's history.

⸎ LEGAL ROW OVER FOOTPATH ⸎

What one newspaper described as the 'genteel atmosphere of Clifton' was disturbed when one of its residents took the law into his own hands to stop what he considered was an invasion of his property.

At the centre of a long-running dispute was a path that ran between two properties, both owned by William Mathias. Although this path was a public right of way, Mathias refused to allow carriages to use it. He waged a war for a number of years, trying to stop anyone riding on the path from Boyce's Avenue to Victoria Square. Mathias even built a wall to block the path, but this was pulled down by objectors. No matter how many times he rebuilt the wall it came down just as quick as it went up, normally under cover of darkness. Eventually Mathias, who became known locally as 'The General', built a stone arch over the path and installed an iron gate.

He must have spent a fortune with lawyers, as he tried to prove his claims in the law courts, including several where he took on Bristol Corporation, who backed the objectors.

The whole affair came to a ludicrous conclusion. A mother, having lifted her new-fangled perambulator over the gate, claimed that Mathias physically pushed her and verbally attacked her. He was accused of assault and the legal battle that ensued became one of semantics. It was a field day for lawyers, as they argued about whether a baby carriage could be interpreted as a carriage under the meaning of the law. Eventually the case was withdrawn, but Mathias continued his campaign.

In 1861, he was sent to prison for six months, for contempt of court. He was by then 92 years old and penniless. On his release from gaol, he sold both his houses and moved. But his arch and an iron gate are still there.

M

❧ 'MAD MINISTER'S CRIME' ❧

According to an old saying, bad news travels fast. That certainly was true when a most bizarre tragedy hit the quiet village of Winterbourne, 8 miles north of Bristol, in July 1906. Shortly after the discovery of the bodies of three people lying in blood in the local church minister's villa in Dragon Road, the news had travelled at least halfway round the world.

In the South Australia capital of Adelaide, *The Advertiser* newspaper carried the simple but shocking headline, 'Mad Minister's Crime'. Underneath, it described the grim scene that the Revd Henry Alban Brown's housekeeper found when she turned up for work one morning. The body of the minister's sister-in-law, Miss Mary Ryder Elliot, was lying dead in a pool of blood. Her throat had been cut with a razor. The terrified domestic ran to the police station and hurried back with a constable. They found not only Miss Elliot's body but also those of the minister and his wife, Maria, in another room. Mrs Brown was wearing a nightdress and seated in a chair. Her husband, wearing a nightshirt, was lying nearby on the floor with his throat also cut. A broken and bloodstained razor was lying on his dressing table. Police found signs that indicated there had been a struggle before the women lost their lives. The Australian newspaper claimed that Mr Brown 'suddenly went mad during the very early hours'.

Revd Brown had been minister at Whiteshill Congregational Chapel in Winterbourne for sixteen years. He had formerly been a solicitor in practice at Haverfordwest with his brother, but gave up the law for the church and trained at the Bristol Theological College.

An inquest into the deaths of the three people heard that the minister had not been feeling his normal self for some time and was on leave from the church, suffering from melancholia, which had led to insomnia. For many nights his wife had kept vigil with him. Mr Brown was seeing two specalists for help.

It was assumed that he had killed his wife first, then his sister-in-law before committing suicide. The coroner recorded a verdict of 'wilful murder' of the two sisters and that Mr Brown had committed suicide 'whilst of unsound mind concerning himself'.

⚜ THE MAN WHO THOUGHT HE WAS THE MESSIAH ⚜

James Naylor was a prominent travelling Quaker evangelist. He was known for his oratory and often spoke out against slavery. He achieved national notoriety when he re-enacted Christ's entry into Jerusalem on Palm Sunday.

He arrived in Bristol one day in October 1656, riding a donkey with half a dozen of his followers chanting 'Holy, Holy, Holy' and 'Hosanna'. They threw garments in front of the horse to cover the muddy path. Naylor was arrested at the White Lion Hotel in Broad Street (on the site of the present Grand Hotel) and taken to London, where he was put on trial before the Second Protectorate Parliament.

Although Naylor claimed that his actions were symbolic, he was convicted of blasphemy. He was ordered to be pilloried and whipped through the streets of London. Naylor was also branded with the letter 'B' on his forehead, to mark him out as a blasphemer, and his tongue was pierced with a hot iron. As if that was not enough punishment, he was sent back to Bristol, where he was whipped through the streets for a second time. After that, he had to serve two years' hard labour in Bridewell prison in London.

Naylor was released from prison a ruined man. On his way back to the family home in Yorkshire, he was robbed and died the next day, aged 42.

⚜ MAYORAL CHAINS ⚜

It's probably not surprising that Bristol has a magnificent collection of civic insignia. After all, it was once the second city in the country after London, and many of its civic customs and ceremonies closely follow those of the capital.

From the thirteenth century, for example, the first citizen – then known as the mayor but since 1899 as Lord Mayor – was given the right to have a sword carried in front of him on civic occasions. Indeed, there are four processional swords, with the oldest dating back to 1373, when Bristol was granted county status.

The official regalia of the Lord Mayor, whose diary is packed with about 1,000 engagements during the year, dates from medieval days. It includes a scarlet robe edged in fur, a feathered tricorn hat, gauntlets and a gold chain of office weighing nearly 3lbs. On occasion, velvets and a dress sword, the correct outfit three centuries ago for men of distinction appearing at Court, are the order of the day.

But, rather curiously, until the middle of the 1920s civic officials don't seem to have given much thought to how the Lady Mayoress was dressed in public. Yet she was carrying out an increasing number of engagements, both with the Lord Mayor and by herself.

It was in 1926 that the council's treasurer, the town clerk and a group of councillors met to discuss the situation. They decided to launch an appeal to the women of

Bristol to raise funds for a specially designed chain of office. Financial contributions came from individuals across the city as well organisations like the Ladies Auxiliary of the Bristol Rotary Club. Enough money came in for the councillors to commission a local jeweller to design and make the chain. It consists of five gold strands which join together with a gold medallion encrusted with fifty-one diamonds and forty-nine sapphires. The medallion is set in a ring of gold surrounded by jewels. Inscribed on the back are the words 'From the women of Bristol'.

The chains of both the Lord Mayor and Lady Mayoress are kept securely under lock and key when not being worn and if the civic dignitaries make any official visits overseas, they wear specially made pendants instead.

❖ MUSTARD GAS FACTORY ❖

During the First World War, the government built a factory near Avonmouth, which operated under top security conditions and even had its own hospital and railway station. It had a workforce of 1,100 people, mostly women and girls, who must have been working in appalling conditions. They had to sign the Official Secrets Act, when they were recruited.

It is still rarely known that this was the United Kingdom's main centre for the manufacture of deadly mustard gas. It was turning out something like 20 tons of the chemical every day.

Mustard gas is a colourless, oily liquid whose vapour is a powerful irritant. It can affect skin and the lungs, causing blistering and even a slow, painful death. It was used in chemical weapons in times of war; in the First World War particularly, the gas could be absorbed by clothing and equipment, making it impossible to protect against. It was first used by the German Army in September 1917. The British government decided to fight back with like for like – hence the factory near Avonmouth.

The difficult and dangerous job of making the gas caused the deaths of three people, because of accidents at the factory. Four others died as a result of their illnesses. At the end of 1918, the factory's medical officer reported a total of 1,400 illnesses amongst the workforce. They suffered from burns, gastritis, mental health problems and bronchopneumonia. The hazardous nature of the gas also meant that people living at Avonmouth were banned from picking blackberries within a mile of the factory. Ironically, the mustard gas made at Avonmouth and despatched by train arrived in France less than two months before the Armistice.

The factory has long been demolished, but the people who live and work nearby now face other hazards, for one of the country's largest concentrations of petrochemical industries is based here.

⚜ A NELSONIAN MYSTERY ⚜

When Admiral Horatio Nelson led the British fleet to victory at the Battle of Trafalgar in 1805, the men of Bristol played their part too. The crew list names at least twenty-four men known to have come from the city.

One of them was Captain Joseph Seymour, who served on HMS *Conqueror*, part of Nelson's fleet. Seymour survived the Battle of Trafalgar and retired to live with his daughter in Bristol. He died at the age of 84 and was buried at Arnos Vale cemetery.

But mystery surrounds one Jemmy Phillips, from North Street in Bedminster. When he died in 1818, the *Bristol Gazette* claimed that he was the boatswain on HMS *Victory* at Trafalgar. According to the paper he 'proved his devotion to his gallant admiral by his numerous wounds including four large sabre wounds on his head'. The paper reported that Philips had many gunshot wounds 'in his body, one right through that went out near the spine and three balls in his right thigh and leg'. It went on to say that 'after the memorable battle of Trafalgar, where he evinced his bravery as boatswain on The Victory, he obtained an honourable discharge'.

In a report of his funeral, the *Bristol Gazette* informed its readers that the streets of the city were lined by thousands of people who wanted to pay their final respects, as the hearse made its way to St Mary Redcliffe church. According to the paper, this 'gallant veteran's remains were towed to their last moorings in the churchyard and saluted with muffled peals by the bells'. His grave is marked by an elaborate and large tabletop monument.

But doubts about the authenticity of Phillips' career have been raised by the Official Nelson Commemoration Committee. They argue that there was 'no Jemmy Phillips serving on The Victory, or indeed any other vessel at the Battle of Trafalgar'. Apparently the only two boatswains of the same surname in Nelson's fleet were John Phillips in HMS *Defence* and William Phillips, acting boatswain in HMS *Euryalus*.

So was Jemmy Phillip's Bristol's biggest hoaxer?

Perched on the top of Nelson's Column in Trafalgar Square, London, is a statue of the admiral. It was cast by Edward Hodges Bailey, a sculptor born in Downend. He attended Bristol Grammar School, where he lightened the routine of lessons for his classmates by modelling wax portraits of them.

⁂ NIPPER'S CLAIM TO FAME ⁂

Nipper, a Jack Russell puppy, was so named because of his tendency to nip the backs of peoples' legs, but his greater claim to fame was that of being a worldwide trademark.

He was the constant companion of his owner, Mark Barraud, a scenic designer, at the Princes Theatre on Park Row, which was destroyed in the Bristol Blitz. When Mark died his brother, Francis, gave Nipper a home. He painted him listening to an early horn gramophone. Francis tried to sell the painting to the firm whose product was featured, but they were not interested. He then offered it to the newly formed Gramophone Company, who agreed to buy the painting if the gramophone was painted out and one of its own models substituted. Francis Barraud agreed, and the firm added the words 'His Master's Voice' to the picture. It quickly became one of the best-known logos in the world.

Nipper first appeared in an advertisement in 1901 and went on to star in magazines, paperweights and on ashtrays and record labels. His picture appeared on records of the top stars of the time, including the Italian tenor Caruso and English band leader and impresario Jack Hylton. Their records were bought by fans around the world and so Nipper's fame spread beyond the British shores.

When he died after being a faithful friend to his two owners for twenty-one years, Francis Barraud buried him in the garden of his home in Surrey.

⁺⁶⁄⁶ OBSERVATORY SEES ALL ⁹⁄₃⁺

Standing on the site of an Iron Age camp 338ft above sea level and overlooking the Clifton Suspension Bridge is one of the country's most unusual buildings. The round tower standing on the hill above the bridge and Avon Gorge is an observatory, which houses the only camera obscura in England.

The building was originally a sixteenth-century windmill. It was partly destroyed by fire, caused by its sails turning furiously during a gale in 1777, becoming overheated. Some fifty years later William West, an artist known for his paintings of the Avon Gorge, rented the ruins from the owners, the Society of Merchant Venturers, for 5s a year.

Besides turning the tower into his home, West, who was also interested in astronomy, equipped it with telescopes, a wind gauge and various other instruments. He also fixed a camera obscura on top of the tower. With a 5in-diameter lens and mirror, it still projects a 360-degree panoramic view on to a white 5ft-diameter bowl-shaped viewing table in a darkened room below.

Clifton Observatory (Janet Naylor)

A 1950s advertisement described the camera:

> The camera obscura to those unacquainted with it has a magical effect. The movement of
> persons, animals and vehicles, the coming and going of ships being brought into the picture
> with distinction and vivid colouring of nature and affording a high gratification to the
> observer, with continual changes and varying effects of light and shade upon the landscape.

West was not a man who let the grass grow under his feet, for he also found time to excavate by blasting and boring through the hard limestone of the Avon Gorge, a 200ft-long tunnel below his observatory. It took him two years to cut the steps to create a passage to a large vault, known as St Vincent's Cave. A viewing platform jutting out from the rock face some 200ft above the River Avon was also installed.

West died in 1861, but his relatives continued living in the Grade II listed building until 1943. Sometime later, the Merchant Venturers sold the observatory, which is now in private ownership. Both the camera obscura and the viewing platform are still popular tourist attractions.

⚜ 'OLD GLORY' FLIES OVER BRISTOL ⚜

On the Fourth of July every year 'Old Glory', or the 'Stars and Stripes' as the American flag is often called, flies from a leafy corner of Clifton. It recalls the days when American troops moved into Clifton College to work on one of the biggest operations of the Second World War. They were engaged in the detailed planning of the D-Day landings, when in June 1944 the world's largest-ever landing fleet would go ashore at Normandy to begin the Nazi defeat of Germany.

During the early days of the war, relatively few bombs were dropped on Clifton. But after a stick of explosives landed near an air-raid shelter in the grounds of Clifton College in December 1940, the school's governors decided that the boys should be moved to safer accommodation. Boys in the prep school were taken to historic Butcombe Court in North Somerset, while the upper school moved into hotels in the North Cornwall resort of Bude.

In their place at Clifton came dozens of American troops, who took over various college buildings. The first Americans arrived in 1942 and by D-Day their numbers had grown to more than 300. They were joined by General Omar Bradley, who arrived from the Mediterranean, where he had commanded II Corps in Sicily.

He took over the housemaster's drawing room in School House, while the college's Council Room became the war room; filled with maps, charts and files of intelligence data. The college's Wilson Tower, named after a former headmaster, became a communications centre for information coming in from the Enigma codebreakers working at such places as Bletchley Park, Buckinghamshire. A housemaster's study was used as a planning room, while classrooms were also put to military use. Many of the college's boarding houses in nearby streets were used as billets for the troops.

When the Americans moved out, a flag which they had flown from the Wilson Tower was given to the college. It was placed in a glass cabinet and put on display. After the war General Bradley was made an honorary Old Cliftonian.

In 1953 he returned to England to represent President Eisenhower at Queen Elizabeth II's coronation. He found time to visit Clifton College and asked that 'Old Glory' should be flown from the Wilson Tower on American Independence Day every year. It is a request that the college still faithfully complies with.

After Hawaii became the fiftieth state of the United States of America, the college was presented with an updated flag. It had earlier been flown from the Capitol building in Washington.

P

❦ PADDLING FOR PLEASURE ❦

The rotting mud-caked timbers of a pier standing in the River Avon are a reminder of more leisurely times; when families went by paddle steamer for excursions to seaside resorts.

For tens of thousands of people, the pier at Hotwells was the starting point of their day trip as they boarded steamers with names like *Glen Avon, Glen Usk* and *Britannia*. The salty tang of the sea was never far away as the steamers headed for Ilfracombe, Weston-super-Mare, Clevedon and Portishead on the Devon and Somerset coast and Barry, Porthcawl and Tenby in South Wales.

The firm of P & A Campbell was the main steamer operator in the Bristol Channel, with its local headquarters in offices close to the Hotwells pier and overlooking the harbour at the Cumberland Basin. Campbell's named their offices Britannia Buildings, after one of the ships in their White Funnel Fleet.

A paddle steamer from that fleet was first seen at Hotwells in 1887. Captain Bob Campbell, a ferry owner on the Clyde, chartered his new paddle steamer, *Waverley*, to a group of Bristol businessmen and sent her south under the command of his son Alec.

The venture was so successful that when Captain Bob died the following year, Alec and his brother transferred their entire business to the Bristol Channel. For many years

The remains of the Hotwells landing stage for paddle steamers (Trevor Naylor)

The paddle steamer *Britannia* about to pass under the Clifton Suspension Bridge (Courtesy of Mildred and Francis Ford)

the firm faced intense competition from rival operators, but passengers preferred the Campbell's steamers, saying they were faster, smarter and more comfortable than all the others. Many trippers regarded the *Bristol Queen* as the pride of the fleet. This was the first Campbell steamer to be built in Bristol and its new features included concealed paddle-boxes, two full-sized masts and oil-fired boilers. The *Bristol Queen* was also the first steamer in the fleet to be given a local name. She first went to sea in 1946 and saw twenty-two years' service before going to a breaker's yard.

Disaster hit the *Glen Usk*, though, when she ran aground at the notorious Horsehoe Bend in the Avon Gorge in 1959. The steamer, on an evening trip to Clevedon, Cardiff and Penarth, had caught the tide while it was ebbing. The 550 passengers on board had to scramble ashore over the rocks to a fleet of buses, which took them home. The *Glen Usk* was refloated the next day and taken away for repairs.

A variety of reasons were to blame for a post-war decline in trade for the steamers. There was the increase in the number of family saloons coming off the production lines of the motor manufacturers, and the opening of the first Severn Bridge in 1966, which gave local people a quick route into Wales. Another factor was rising operational costs, and fuel charges in particular. On top of all this, Campbell's faced another major blow with the collapse of Clevedon Pier during safety tests in 1971. It meant that steamers could no longer call at the North Somerset resort.

So perhaps it should not have been a surprise when in that same year the firm announced it would be abandoning regular passenger sailings from Bristol, Weston, and Barry. Campbell's also closed their offices at Hotwells.

Ships in the White Funnel Fleet were veterans of both world wars. During the Second World War, they went into the Charles Hill shipyard at Albion Dock to be stripped of all their seating before going off to be refitted as minesweepers. Their white paint and funnels were changed to drab grey for military life, and their names altered to avoid confusion with existing naval ships.

Less than half of the entire fleet of twelve steamers returned to home waters after the Second World War. Some had been sunk and others beached or lost in appalling weather conditions.

⚜ PAY ON THE NAIL ⚜

Many of the phrases that are used in everyday language come from the Bible or Shakespeare, but Bristol is believed to be the birthplace of at least one popular saying.

A Bristol Nail in Corn Street (Trevor Naylor)

Outside the eighteenth-century Exchange building in Corn Street, built by John Wood the Elder who did so much to beautify Bath, stand four brass pillars known as the Bristol Nails. They are much older than the Exchange itself and had previously been situated in another part of the street. These 4cwt pillars were used by merchants to seal their business deals and count their money. The circular tops of each pillar have raised edges that prevent coins rolling on to the pavement. It is said that this led to the coining of the phrase 'pay on the nail'.

The first nail, near All Saints church, is the oldest, being of the late Elizabethan period. The second was the gift of Alderman Robert Kitchin, one time Mayor of Bristol, who died in 1594. The third nail was made by Thomas Hobson of Bristol but was given to the city by Nicholas Crisp, a London businessman. The last nail, dated 1631, was the gift of George White, a local merchant and brother of Dr Thomas White, who founded an almshouse which is still running under his name.

In 1813, a twice-weekly corn market was held at the Exchange. At one time, corn merchants would leave the building to show potential buyers their samples on the nails, where the light was brighter. This frequently happened in the 'black-out' days during the Second World War, when windows were covered up to prevent light escaping and thus being a guide to enemy aircraft.

The brass pillars are ornamental today, but they come into their own each November. Presidents of three Colston Societies – The Anchor, The Dolphin and The Grateful – formally exchange cheques on the nails to launch their annual appeals to help the elderly. The societies were formed in the eighteenth century to carry on the philanthropic work of wealthy merchant Edward Colston, who was also involved in the slave trade.

For many years, Wood's Exchange was the place appointed for the nomination of candidates in parliamentary elections and the declaration of the poll result amidst noisy scenes. Today it is a marketplace full of independent traders selling their wares.

✤ PEN PARK HOLE TRAGEDY ✤

As one of the country's largest natural underground cavities, Pen Park Hole has long been a site of exploration. The depth of the cave, on the edge of the Southmead housing estate, is about 200ft with its roof about 12ft below the surface. It occurs in a ridge of carboniferous limestone.

The cave is believed to have been formed by rising geothermal water. Whether it was discovered by quarrying or miners searching for deposits of lead, no one is certain. But the first recorded descent of the cave was made in 1669 by Captain Samuel Sturmy, a Master Mariner living at Easton-in-Gordano, Somerset.

At the bottom of the cavern he found a lake, the depth of which was said to change with the seasons. He described the water as being 'sweet, clear and as good as anything I drank'.

Sturmy became ill four days after his descent and died in a fever.

It was thirteen years later that the second recorded exploration of Pen Park Hole was made. This time, Captain Greenville Collins of the survey yacht *Merlin*, accompanied by his crew, spent two days searching the main chamber and passages leading from it. A report on their findings was published the following year by The Royal Society in London.

Such was the interest in Pen Park Hole that the Revd Thomas Newnham, a 25-year-old Minor Canon at Bristol Cathedral, went there in an attempt to ascertain its depth. He took with him a plumb line and steadied himself by holding the branch of an ash tree. Unfortunately, the ground was wet and slippery and as Mr Newnham dropped the line down the hole, he lost his footing and fell into the pit. Several friends with him, including the woman he was to marry, watched in horror.

In an ironic coincidence, earlier that day Mr Newnham had used as a text for his sermon Psalm No. 88, which contains the words: 'I am counted as one of them that go down to the pit ... thou has laid me in the lowest pit, in a place of darkness and in the deep.'

Although repeated efforts were made to rescue Mr Newnham's body, it was not recovered for another six weeks, when it was found floating on the top of the lake.

The entrance to Pen Park Hole, which is on land owned by Bristol City Council, has long been sealed for safety reasons. Admission is strictly controlled and normally only granted to members of caving clubs.

⚜ PIE POUDRE COURT ⚜

A small wooden sign hanging outside a pub recalls the days when instant justice was dispensed to miscreants.

From the twelfth century onwards, Old Market was the site of a large market and fair, serving the nearby Bristol Castle. It attracted many hundreds of merchants, pedlars and more than its fair share of rogues. Indeed, the market became renowned for its riotous behaviour.

In Norman times, a special court was set up to deal swiftly with the many thieves and debtors who plagued the market. Known as Pie Poudre Court, it was held in the open air under an ancient oak tree, now the site of the Stag & Hounds pub. The court eventually moved inside the pub, sitting in a large panelled room above its portico.

Pie Poudre Court was intended specifically for settling the many disputes that arose at the market. Its name is believed to have come from Old French and loosely translated, means 'dusty foot'. This is a reference to the swiftness with which justice was handed down – before defendants had time to shake the dust off their feet and escape judgement.

The court was last held in 1870, when it was amalgamated with the ancient Saxon Court of the Tolzey, then held at the Guildhall in Broad Street. However, a traditional opening and closing ceremony continued to be enacted outside the Stag & Hounds at the end of every September. The sergeant-at-mace of the Tolzey Court proclaimed the holding of a session of the Court of Pie Poudre with the words:

> All manner of persons having anything to do at this Court of the Tolzey for the City and County of Bristol held and kept here this day in the Old Market, draw near and give your attendance.

After a short pause he closed the proceedings, saying:

> All manner of persons who have anything further to do at this Court of the Tolzey for the City and County of Bristol, held and kept here this day in the Old Market, may now depart hence and give their attendance at the Tolzey Court Office forthwith. God Save the Queen, the Judge of this Court and his Deputy.

At one time, those who officiated at this ceremony were provided with toast and cheese, along with a glass of spiced mead, while the commoners drank beer and cider.

This symbolic tradition of briefly opening and closing the court was abandoned in 1973, when there was an overhaul of the English court system. All that is left is the pub sign, which simply states that the pub was the site of an ancient court.

The Stag & Hounds was probably built as a private house with four plain pillars supporting the first floor and forming a portico over the pavement. The first record of the building being licensed premises is 1815. A magnificent Jacobean seventeenth-century staircase still exists, although for many years it has been hidden from public view.

During alterations in the 1980s, an 8ft-deep well which once supplied water for the pub's own brewery was discovered. It is now a feature of the bar. Once hemmed in on all sides by shops and houses, the pub now stands on the edge of a traffic-clogged roundabout and underpass.

❧ PORTISHEAD IS BORN AGAIN ❧

There was a time when the aldermen and councillors of Bristol had their eyes set on developing the North Somerset coastal town of Portishead, 9 miles south of the city. Way back since the seventeenth century they had been gradually adding to their estate, initially taking ownership of the manors of North Weston and Portishead.

By the early nineteenth century they had grand plans to turn Portishead, then a fishing village, into a popular seaside resort; a place where wealthy businessmen could live away from the smoke and noise of industrial Bristol.

The councillors and aldermen built the Royal Pier Hotel on land they owned near the pier. It was opened in 1831 and is thought to the only seaside hotel built by a public authority at the time. It was sold in the 1970s, and today carries on life as the Royal Inn, a privately run venture.

In 1905 Bristol Corporation commissioned the golfer Harry Vardon, six-time winner of the British Open and also a winner of the US Open, to design a golf course for the growing resort. He produced plans for an 18-hole course on 83 acres of land at Nore Road, running alongside the Bristol Channel. Two dozen unemployed men in Bristol were taken on to build the course, which was officially opened by the Lord Mayor of Bristol in July 1907. Following the formal speeches, Harry Vardon and J.H. Taylor, another British Open winner, staged an exhibition match.

The golf course was leased for fifteen years to a group of men who styled themselves as Portishead Golf Club Ltd, initially paying £100 a year with five-yearly rental reviews. Ten days after the opening celebrations, the first recorded club match took place against Henbury Golf Club from Bristol, with a victory for the Portishead Club.

In both the First and Second World Wars, parts of the course were turned over to growing vegetables. The clubhouse, which incorporated an old windmill, was also used by the Home Guard as their local base.

Over the years, various organisations have run the golf course, with the Bristol council eventually selling off part of the land for homes. The rest of the site has also changed hands; an Approach Golf Course now runs there.

Meanwhile, Portishead has become one of the fastest-growing towns in Europe, with thousands of homes, shops and offices being developed in recent years, creating a whole new environment. Instead of becoming a major seaside resort, it is now a dormitory town for Bristol.

❧ THE PRINCESS WHO WAS A FAKE ❧

On the evening of Maundy Thursday in 1817, a young woman wearing colourful Eastern dress was seen wandering through the sleepy village of Almondsbury, 8 miles north of Bristol. She was wearing a black stuff gown with a muslin frill at the neck, a red and black shawl around her shoulders, and a black cotton shawl on her head. She carried a small bundle on her arm containing a few necessities, including soap.

Villagers watched as the woman, in her mid–20s, knocked at the door of a cottage and uttered strange words to the owners. She talked in a language that no one could understand, but by her signs the owner realised that she was asking for food and shelter. He took her to Knole Park House, the home of Samuel Worrall, the Town Clerk of Bristol and a magistrate. Being kindly people, he and his wife, Elizabeth, gave the woman hospitality. They tried to discover her background, but to no avail. She had some curious habits, including going on to the roof of the Worralls' home to pray. The woman apparently called herself Caraboo and only drank tea and ate vegetables.

Mr Worrall asked her to write down her native script, which he sent to Oxford University for examination. Academics there described it as a 'humbug language' and treated it as a joke.

The woman was taken to Bristol to be examined by the mayor and then on to St Peter's Hospital, which cared for vagrants. However, she caused so many problems there that she was sent back to the Worralls' home. Despite this, they introduced her to Bristol society and she became something of a celebrity. A ball in her honour was even held in Bath. By now, the stranger was being treated like a visiting head of state.

She was introduced to a Portuguese sailor, who could apparently understand her language. The woman claimed to be Princess Caraboo of Javasu, an island in the Indian Ocean. Her story was that she had been kidnapped from her home by pirates and held captive on their ship. She claimed to have escaped by jumping overboard into the Bristol Channel and swimming ashore.

'Princess Caraboo' danced exotically for the magistrate's friends and even swam naked in a lake when she was on her own. By all accounts, she was having a wonderful time until the landlady of a boarding house in Bristol recognised the description of the woman in a newspaper report. She had provided her with lodgings some six months earlier.

When confronted by her landlady, Princess Caraboo had no trouble speaking English. Her ruse, which had gone on for three months, was over. It transpired that the self-styled princess was really Mary Wilcocks, who came from Witheridge in Devon. She was no princess, but the daughter of a cobbler. Apparently, she adopted the disguise in the hope that it would make her more interesting.

Mary Wilcocks expressed a wish to go to America, so Mrs Worrall arranged for her passage to Philadelphia, accompanied by a chaperone. The journey, however, was not uneventful. It was reported in *Felix Farley's Bristol Journal* that Mary Wilcocks had gone ashore at St Helena, where she met Napoleon. He was said to have found her 'enchanting'.

Mary stayed in America for seven years before returning to England. She made one last appearance as Princess Caraboo in a London gallery, where she charged visitors a shilling to see her. The fake princess then returned to Bristol, setting up business in Bedminster as an importer and seller of leeches, then an important medical commodity. One of her clients was the Bristol Infirmary.

When Mary Wilcocks died in 1864 at the age of 75, she was buried in an unmarked grave in Hebron Churchyard, Southville. Her daughter Mary Ann carried on the business of selling leeches.

❧ 'QUEEN OF SUBURBS' ❧

The Poet Laureate John Betjeman once described Clifton as 'the queen of suburbs'. He was impressed by the Georgian squares, terraces and mansions built by prosperous merchants who were intent on moving away from the industrial grime and pollution of the city. Many of these mansions – like Clifton Hill House, the Bishop's Palace and Goldney House – still survive.

From about 1780, a building boom took place in Britain, and work started on many of Clifton's terraces and crescents. However, the Napoleonic Wars caused a depression and more than one Clifton developer went bankrupt.

Construction of Royal York Crescent for example, reputed to be the longest crescent in Europe at just under a quarter of a mile long, started in 1791 but came to a standstill two years later. It wasn't completed until 1820. The builders

Royal York Crescent, Clifton (Janet Naylor)

The retaining wall of Windsor Terrace, built by William Watts (Trevor Naylor)

of the crescent may well have been superstitious, for they did not include a No. 13, preferring 12a instead. At one stage the government bought the site, along with the unfinished part of the crescent, planning to build military barracks there. Their scheme met strong opposition from local people and it never came to fruition.

Clifton attracted a number of speculators who tried their hand at property development. One of them was William Watts, a plumber, who had been successfully involved in the manufacture of lead shot. Watts had turned his home on Redcliffe Hill into the world's first lead shot tower, by taking the roof off and replacing it with a castellated tower. This enabled him to pour molten lead from a great height through a perforated zinc pan so that it fell into a tank of water in the cellar, making perfectly spherical shot without any pimples or scratches. Watts sold his patent for making lead shot in 1790 for £10,000 and went on to build a terrace of up to twenty houses standing on an escarpment, more than 200ft above the streets below.

To ensure that what became Windsor Terrace was safe, he had to construct a massive retaining wall close to the sheer face of the cliffs of the Avon Gorge. The cost of the foundations alone used up the money he received for his patent. Watts was made bankrupt, and ever since the wall has been known as Watts Folly.

Another developer, John Drew, went on to complete the terrace. Afterwards he moved on to build a cul-de-sac of fifteen houses nearby, which was called The Paragon. While the fronts of the houses are concave, the porches, with

The Paragon, Clifton (Janet Naylor)

The shot tower that stood on Redcliffe Hill
(Author's collection)

their double front doors, curve the other way. It's the only street in Bristol with curved porches. However, Drew went bankrupt and another developer took over, who in turn also lost his money, but not before building one of the houses with a ballroom. Untouched by modernity, the houses in The Paragon, all Grade II listed, both inside and out, stand as a splendid example of Georgian domestic architecture.

Meanwhile, Watts' shot tower was still in business until 1968, when it was demolished to make way for road widening. Although the building was classified as a Grade II listed building of architectural or historical importance, the local planners decided that it could fall into the mouth of the bulldozer. They claimed it was of a poor architectural condition and had deteriorated badly.

✤ QUEEN OPENS HOSPITAL AT ARM'S LENGTH ✤

When a queen comes to town to open a new building, everyone expects her to cut a ceremonial tape, unveil a commemorative plaque, say a few gracious words and take a guided tour of the building. However, none of that happened when Queen Victoria, along with her entourage, rolled into Bristol in November 1899 for her first visit to the city in seventy years.

The city fathers certainly laid on the red carpet treatment with much style. From the moment Her Majesty stepped off her train at Temple Meads station she found every street through which her carriage passed to be decorated with golden eagles carrying laurel wreaths and millions of flowers in elaborate arrangements. The royal procession to Clifton included nine carriages, mounted police and a foot party of soldiers.

To mark the occasion, a fireworks display which cost £300 was staged on Clifton Downs while another £1,500 was spent on commemorative medals and refreshments for 60,000 children, many of whom lined the streets to get a glimpse of Her Majesty. Another 26,000 youngsters lined up on the Downs to form a choir which sang the National Anthem.

Queen Victoria was in town to open a new convalescent home, the Queen Victoria Hospital, which had been built overlooking Clifton Downs. The elegant building had been a private school but a public subscription fund was opened so that it could be converted into a convalescent home with eighty beds. By the time of the official opening, generous citizens had contributed £100,000.

But if they were expecting to see the royal personage walking up the steps to the building's front door, they were disappointed. The queen did not leave her carriage to carry out the official opening ceremony. Instead she pressed a button on her lap to which an electric wire was attached. The next morning, the *Western Daily Press* reported that 'this [the button] brought into operation an electric magnet with sufficient power to raise a clutch on the door and then the released door flew open'. The same electrical current also set the building's turret clock working. The Queen did not tour the home, but the newspaper reported her as describing it as 'noble'.

On the same day, Queen Victoria knighted Bristol's first Lord Mayor, Herbert Ashman (*see* Civic Customs), again without leaving her carriage. With a borrowed sword she dubbed him on the shoulder while leaning out of the carriage which had conveniently stopped outside the Council House, then in Corn Street.

No explanation was offered for this but presumably the frail and aged queen, who died two years later aged 81, preferred the comfort of her carriage to standing in the cold.

❧ QUEEN'S PRAISE FOR CHURCH ☙

On her visit to Bristol in 1574, Queen Elizabeth I is reputed to have described St Mary Redcliffe church as 'the fairest, goodliest and most famous parish church in England'. Unfortunately, there is no documentary evidence, not even a single line in the church records, to support this remark and equally nothing to disprove it.

However, if Elizabeth I did utter these words, it would have been rather odd of her to do so. It could well be argued that she did not see the church at its finest, for two-thirds of its cloud-piercing spire had crashed across the roof of the nave during a thunderstorm more than a century earlier. Financial circumstances meant that the spire was not replaced until 1882.

It wasn't until 1848 that the Canynges Society, or Friends of St Mary Redcliffe, was formed to raise funds for the restoration of the church. The final act of that restoration was the laying of the capstone, weighing about 1 ton, on the top of the new spire. By then the society had raised £14,179 towards the restoration, which cost some £40,000.

St Mary Redcliffe church at its finest (Author's collection)

The *Bristol Times and Mirror* reported that the mayor, Mr William Proctor Baker, and his wife, the mayoress, accepted a most unusual invitation from the vicar of Redcliffe church. It was to lay the capstone almost 300ft above street level. The ceremony was held on Ascension Day 1872, with the spire still encased in scaffolding. It was reported that the only way for the civic couple to reach the top was by a series of hoists. 'It was merely two square boards, one overhead and the other under foot, like the top and bottom of a box, with a rope at each corner, covered on three sides with drapery. Into this the Mayoress got, and was hoisted by the workmen to the top of the spire,' said the paper.

After traveling part of the way by hoist, the mayor decided to make the rest of the journey by climbing the wooden ladders attached to the scaffolding. At the top he used a silver trowel, now displayed inside the church, to set the capstone in place with cement. Afterwards he returned to terra firma with his wife and the vicar.

Unfortunately, soft Dundry stone was used in the restoration of the spire and, with its low resistance to air pollution, it soon started to decay. Less than 100 years later further restoration work was required, not just to parts of the spire, but also the exterior of the church.

Two-thirds of the spire collapsed during a storm, leaving a stump (Courtesy of Mildred and Francis Ford)

A benefactor promised to fund the whole cost of restoring the external fabric of the church, which amounted to £100,000. The church, therefore, had to find funds only for the interior repairs. This time Clipsham stone was used, because of its resilience to atmospheric pollution. It had already been used in the restoration of Oxford colleges.

The work at Redcliffe was completed in 1933, when the Archbishop of Canterbury, Dr Cosmo Lang, presided over a special service in which he hallowed the work. He wore a cope and mitre which had been specially made for the service by a member of the Redcliffe congregation.

Bristol could not have seen a service on such a grand scale for many a year. More than forty clergy, including former vicars of Redcliffe, others from churches around the city and eight bishops, joined the archbishop in procession to the chancel. When he offered the 'Great Prayer of Hallowing', every light in the church was extinguished, save for four candles which gleamed about the High Altar. After the service the archbishop went to the steps of the church's north porch to pronounce his blessing upon the 'parish, the port, the city and the diocese'. He was watched by thousands of people who could not gain entry to the service, but had waited several hours outside the church on a cold night to see him.

⚜ QUEEN SQUARE RECLAIMED ⚜

Queen Square, in the heart of the city, is Bristol's oldest open space and was built as a perfect square – all its sides are equal. Before it was developed into a desirable residential area at the start of the eighteenth century, it was known as the boggy Town Marsh. It was laid out as a square and named after Queen Anne in 1702, after she visited the city. She was welcomed by a 100-gun salute.

The centrepiece of the square is an equestrian statue, which many lovers of art regard as a classic example of the work of the Flemish sculptor John Michael Rysbrach. His brass statue of William III was cast at his studio in London and shipped down the Thames to Bristol in 1735. King William is depicted on horseback, unusually without stirrups, and wearing Roman costume. The statue is mounted on a plain Portland stone pedestal in the centre of Queen Square.

In the 1930s it was moved when council planners brutally damaged the square by driving the Inner Circuit Road diagonally through it, to link the city centre with Redcliffe Way. When the road was completed, Rysbrach's statue was installed on an island in the middle of the dual carriageway, with cars, buses and lorries roaring past all day. The statue was moved again shortly before the Second World War, when it was taken for safety to the Duke of Beaufort's stately home and park at Badminton in South Gloucestershire. It was returned to Bristol in 1948.

King William III on horseback (Author's collection)

Queen Square was eventually returned to something like its original beauty in time for the millennium celebrations. To much acclaim, the planners removed the road and created footpaths across the square. It meant that William III was on the move once again, this time back to his original site.

The square has been associated with both local and international history. One of its first residents was Captain Woodes Rogers, master of the vessel which brought Alexander Selkirk to Bristol. The Scottish sailor had been marooned in the Juan Fernandez Islands in the South Pacific for four years, after having an argument with his captain.

The story goes that while staying in Bristol, Selkirk met the novelist Daniel Defoe and became the inspiration for his tale *Robinson Crusoe*. It is said that the couple met at the Llandoger Trow, which would have been Woodes Rogers' local pub, just around the corner from his home. Woodes Rogers later became governor of the Isle of Providence in the Bahamas.

In 1792, the first American consulate in Britain was set up in a house on the south side of Queen Square. It was opened to protect the interests of Americans living in Bristol.

The face of Queen Square changed dramatically in 1831, though, when three days of rioting broke out after the House of Lords blocked a popular Electoral Reform Bill. Rioters looted and destroyed many buildings, including the mayor's mansion house and the Customs House. The mob was eventually attacked by armed dragoons and hundreds of people were injured, some fatally.

Being close to the city docks, Queen Square was a natural choice for many shipping firms to have their offices. They moved in alongside the headquarters of the Port of Bristol Authority and the local office of Her Majesty's Customs and Excise. Consuls from many European countries also based themselves here.

However, as ships became bigger, they found it impossible to navigate the Avon Gorge, and so the docks began to make heavy losses. They were closed to commercial shipping by the city council in the 1970s. Marine-related businesses in Queen Square moved out and have since been replaced by barristers, solicitors, accountants and other professionals.

The square though, may be turning full circle as one or two of the houses have since reverted to family homes.

⚜ RAILWAY THROUGH THE ROCKS ⚜

Clifton Rocks Railway was probably way ahead of its time. If it were running now it would certainly help to ease the city's traffic congestion, as well as being a major tourist attraction. It was built by George Newnes, MP, publisher and entrepreneur. To him, a funicular railway was nothing new. He had already largely financed and built a cliff railway which linked the Devon towns of Lynmouth, on the shoreline, and Lynton, on the cliff top. But the Clifton railway was something different. To preserve the grandeur of the Avon Gorge, it had to be built inside the rocks.

As owners of large tracts of land and property in Clifton, the Society of Merchant Venturers allowed Newnes to go ahead with the railway, but they imposed a condition. They required him to build a hydropathic institution with a pump room next door to the railway's Clifton station. They visualised this as being a successor to the Hotwells spa.

Building the railway was a most difficult engineering feat, for a 450ft-long tunnel had to be blasted and cut through hard limestone. The tunnel, with a vertical rise of 1ft for every 2.2ft, forms a straight and direct link between the Clifton station and the one at Hotwells. This was close to the landing stage for paddle steamers, the rail link to Avonmouth and the trams that trundled into the city centre.

It took Newnes two years to build the railway – workmen were often hampered by rock falls – complete with its two tracks at a cost of £30,000. It operated on a water balance system. This involved filling the tanks of the passenger carriages at the Clifton station with enough water to raise those at the Hotwells level. The tanks were emptied at the bottom and water pumped up to the top; a cycle which was continuously repeated.

The railway was opened amid much celebration in March 1893. On the first day, 6,220 people made the return journey. At the end of the first six weeks of operation, more than 100,000 passengers had passed through the turnstiles. Such was the railway's popularity that by the end of its first year, 427,492 people had bought a ticket for the forty-four-second ride. Clifton Rocks Railway busiest day came on 5 July 1913, when 14,000 people used it to visit the Royal Show, an agricultural event, which was staged on Clifton Downs.

The Hotwells station of the Clifton Rocks Railway (Author's collection)

The Clifton (top) station (Janet Naylor)

The blue and white carriages, which could each seat up to eighteen passengers, ran up and down the tunnel for nearly four decades. Passenger numbers started to drop, though, with the opening of the Portway, the A4 road that links Bristol with Avonmouth Docks. The arterial road ran close to the Hotwells station, making it difficult for passengers to reach the paddle steamers on the opposite side of the road. The end of the line for the Rocks Railway came with its closure in 1934. The carriages were lowered to the Hotwells station and eventually removed.

However, the Second World War gave the tunnel new and unexpected uses. The BBC wanted to ensure that its programmes stayed on air during the war and took over part of the tunnel for a transmitter station. The British Overseas Airways Corporation, now British Airways, moved out of London for the duration of the war and took over the top part of the tunnel, for barrage balloon repairs, and also moved their head office there. The airline also took over part of the hotel next door.

Clifton Rocks Railway is largely forgotten by Bristolians today, save for an enthusiastic band of volunteers who are restoring the Clifton station and have ambitious but costly plans of one day reopening the railway, with possibly one or two cars instead of the original four.

⁂ RED MAIDS' ON THE MARCH ⁂

Every autumn, 600 girls wearing red bring a splash of colour to the city centre as they celebrate their school's Founder's Day. But this is not a traditional anniversary marking the birth or the death of the founder, or even the day the school opened. Instead, the students of Red Maids' School are celebrating their founder's survival of an attack on his life.

John Whitson was born in the Forest of Dean in about 1555. He came to Bristol as a teenager with nothing. However, this did not prevent him from becoming one of the city's most colourful and influential self-made men. Starting work as an apprentice to a wine merchant, he rose to become a Member of Parliament (being elected four times), Mayor of Bristol (twice) and Master of the Society of Merchant Venturers (also twice). He married three times, each time to a widow.

It was on 7 November (Julian calendar) 1626 that Whitson (by now an alderman) was stabbed in the face by Christopher Callowhill. The attack happened when Whitson was sitting in court, trying to settle a dispute between Callowhill and another man. He was stabbed with a knife, which went through his nose and cheek into his mouth.

Whitson made a remarkable recovery from his injuries, and to commemorate this, he left funds in his will for a sermon to be preached at St Nicholas church each year. When he died three years later after a fall from his horse, Whitson, a wealthy merchant, endowed Red Maids' School. He left £90 a year to provide 'a fit convenient dwelling house' for 'one grave, painful and modest woman ... and for forty poor women children whose parents shall be deceased or decayed'.

In his will he left instructions that the girls should be taught to read and sew, or do some other laudable work. Whitson stipulated that they were to 'have double apparel provided always and be apparelled in red cloth'.

Red Maids' Hospital, as it started out in life, opened on College Green in 1634, making it the oldest girls' school in the country. Later, the school moved to premises in nearby Denmark Street and just over 100 years ago it moved again, to its present site in its own grounds at Westbury-on-Trym.

Founder's Day starts with a candlelit memorial service in the crypt of St Nicholas church, where the school's head girls place a wreath on Whitson's tomb. The whole school, dressed in red, then marches across the city centre to Bristol Cathedral for a thanksgiving service. This is one of the biggest processions the city sees each year, as it brings traffic to a halt.

⚜ RINGING THE CHANGES ⚜

When Queen Elizabeth I made a week-long visit to Bristol in 1574 on one of her royal progresses around her realm, the bells of St Stephen's church pealed out to greet her. The monarch was said to have been so charmed by the sound coming from the church's elegant perpendicular tower that she promised the ringers a royal charter. Unfortunately, it never quite materialised. However, that has never deterred members of the Antient (they prefer the old spelling of 'ancient') Society of St Stephen's Ringers from greatly honouring Good Queen Bess, right up to the present day.

It is not known when the society was founded, although it is believed to be of pre-Reformation origin. The earliest documentary evidence the society has is a copy of certain ordinances dated 1620, which bound members to curious rules. The wording now seems most quaint, and the penalty for any infringement of the rules quainter still. One of them reads: 'If anyone after the time that he shall come into the church to ring, shall curse or swear, or make any noise or disturbance, either in scoffing or unseemly jesting, the party so offending shall pay for his offence three pence.'

Another rule warned the members that if anyone was to be 'so saucy as to take the rope to ring before the Master ... the party so offending shall pay, for such his offence, two pence – one penny thereof to the Sexton and the other penny to the company'.

It was also made clear to the ringers that 'if any one of the said company shall be so rude as to run into the Belfry before he do kneel down and pray, as every Christian ought to do, he shall pay, for the first offence, six pence, and the second he shall be cast out of the company'.

There is evidence to show that the society was originally one of bell-ringers, pure and simple. Peal boards in the church tower testify to the fact that peals were still being rung under the society's banner into the last twenty years or so of the nineteenth century. But at a meeting in November 1894, chaired by the vicar of St Stephen's, a new organisation for ringers was formed, which went by the name of the St Stephen's Ringers Guild. By the end of the century, the Antient Society of St Stephen's Ringers had become a group of gentlemen to whom the art of bell-ringing was something of a mystery, but who were fond of good company and pleasant gathering.

From then on it seems that the society became a benevolent group of philanthropic businessmen, dedicated to raising funds for the maintenance of this historic church. In recent years its members have been responsible for refurbishing the church café and renovating the church's south porch. Members still faithfully maintain long-standing and some most unusual customs, though. Every year on the Sunday closest to 17 November, the birthday of Queen Elizabeth I, they don morning dress to attend a commemorative service in the church. The following day they continue their tradition of merrymaking at their annual dinner. No ordinary dinner, this, for during the course of the meal the ordinances are read, handbells rung and a ballad that was written in 1788 and called 'The Golden Days of Good Queen Bess' is sung. Each of the twelve verses is allotted to a different member of the society or an honoured guest. The first verse runs:

> To my muse give attention, and deem it not a mystery,
> If we jumble together music, poetry and history,
> The times for to display in the days of good Queen Bess, sir,
> Whose name and royal memory posterity may bless, sir.

After each verse the ringers sing the refrain:

> Oh! The golden days of good Queen Bess!
> Merry be the memory of good Queen Bess!

The society also organises an early morning service to welcome May Day. A pair of sturdy legs is needed for this service, as it takes place on the top of St Stephen's church tower, 133ft above street level. It is a similar service to that held at Magdalen College, Oxford, where for more than 500 years choristers have welcomed the month of May from the top of the Great Tower, singing hymns and madrigals.

St Stephen's church, dating back to the fourteenth century, once stood on the edge of Bristol's docks. Old paintings depict ships moored so close to the church as to be almost touching its walls. Development of the area down the centuries means it is now hemmed in by pubs, restaurants and office blocks, some of which have been converted into residential accommodation.

The parish boundaries of St Stephen's are unusual as they include all of the River Avon (water only, not the land alongside) out to the islands of Steep Holm and Flat Holm in the Severn Estuary.

⁘ ROMAN PORT AT SEA MILLS ⁘

When the Romans invaded Britain, they established a port at what is now Sea Mills. They called it Portus Abonae. ('Abonae' is Celtic for river). It is thought that the port was a disembarkation point for journeys across the River Severn to Wales. It seems that by the fourth century AD, however, the Romans had left the area.

In 1712, Joshua Franklyn, a local merchant, constructed a wet dock on the site of the Roman port. It would save ships making the hazardous journey through the Avon Gorge into the wharves at Bristol. Franklyn founded the Sea Mills Dock Company, which attracted thirty-two investors, but the enterprise was never a success. Poor overland links made it difficult to transport cargoes into Bristol. This meant they had to be taken upriver by barge.

Despite attempts by other merchants to make the dock a viable concern, it was abandoned by the end of the eighteenth century and fell into disrepair. However, some of the harbour walls that Franklyn built can still be seen today.

For many years the River Signal Station on the bank of the Avon, close to Sea Mills Dock, was a landmark to ships' captains navigating their vessels into Bristol. The station, with its round tower, was operated by the Port of Bristol Authority, but modern technology has taken over its role. However the station, with its tower offering a panoramic view of the river, still stands, having become a private house.

⁘ RUGBY CLUB'S STRANGE STORY ⁘

Little could the group of men supping ale around the bar-room table have realised that the rugby club they were forming would become part of Bristol's sporting history, and would still be going strong nearly a century and a half later.

The twenty men who gathered in the King's Arms at the top of Whiteladies Road in 1872 were the founders of Clifton Rugby Club. This was the first rugby club in the city and predates its rival, Bristol Rugby, by sixteen years.

At the inaugural meeting, rules for the game were drawn up. They were largely based on those of Clifton College, which had been founded ten years earlier. Rugby was already a popular sport with the pupils, and at least six of the men at the meeting in the King's Arms had been educated at the college. Enthusiasm to get out on to the pitch was such that Clifton played its first match just a few weeks later, against Sydney College at Bath, and the players returned home with a victory under their belts.

Success didn't seem far from Clifton Rugby Club in its early days. It finished its first season undefeated and in the following four seasons, lost only five matches. A year after being formed, the club took great pride in having its first international player. James Arthur Bush played for England in 1873, in what was then twenty-a-side rugby. He was a former Clifton College boy who also played cricket for Gloucestershire and had been the best man at the wedding of W.G. Grace, who later became known as 'the great cricketing doctor'.

Rather strangely, for a club that was founded in and named after Clifton, it had never played a home game in Clifton in its first 140 years. Over the years the club has led a somewhat nomadic existence, playing in various parts of north Bristol, including Redland, Horfield and Westbury-on-Trym. Its headquarters are now at Cribbs Causeway, just north of the city boundary.

In September 2013, club officials arranged with the headmaster of Clifton College to play on its ground as the 'home' side against Bishops Stortford. Happily for Clifton, which still proudly retains its amateur status and turns out four sides every Saturday, the club defeated the visitors 21–19.

⚜ SCHOOL FOR 'SONS OF GENTLEMEN' ⚜

In the second half of the nineteenth century there was a groundswell of opinion amongst the more ambitious citizens who wanted a school modelled on the lines of Rugby.

They recognised that there were already many private schools in the Clifton area, but regarded them as 'small and ephemeral' and wholly dependent on the circumstances of the individuals who ran them. One such school in Royal York Crescent educated Eugenie Montijo, who became Empress of France, and her sister Paca, later Duchess of Alba. These daughters of a Spanish nobleman were sent to attend a boarding school at Nos 1–3 on the crescent. This was an establishment run by a Mrs Rogers and her daughters which closed in 1855.

A campaign got underway with clergyman, civic dignitaries, businessmen and the literary set, all of whom wanted a public school in Clifton: an establishment where boys could attain the highest branches of learning. Clifton College Company was specifically launched to achieve this aim and issued 400 shares of £25 each. They were quickly taken up by prominent citizens, enabling the company to buy 13 acres of land for £14,000 for the school site. It was immediately behind the Bristol, Clifton and West of England Zoological Society's grounds.

The first prospectus stated that the school was founded for the 'purposes of providing for the Sons of Gentlemen a thoroughly good and liberal education at a modest cost'. Clifton College opened in September 1862 with a special service at which the headmaster John Percival addressed sixty-nine boys. He told them to be 'truthful and manly'. The college chapel hadn't yet been built, so benches were borrowed from the Victoria Rooms and a choir from Bristol Cathedral led the singing. Percival later instructed parents not to give boys too much pocket money; a weekly limit of 1s was set.

It is generally thought that Percival was the first person to be appointed headmaster of Clifton College but he was, in fact, second choice. The Revd Charles Evans, a teacher at Rugby, had earlier been appointed to the post but less than a month before the college was due to open, he resigned. Mr Evans had decided to accept the headship of his own old school, King Edward's in Birmingham, instead.

Clifton College (Trevor Naylor)

Percival was headmaster for sixteen years, during which time he saw the number of pupils rise to 680. He left Clifton to become President of Trinity College, Oxford, and was later appointed Bishop of Hereford.

When he died aged 82, Percival was buried, according to his own instructions, in the vault of the chapel at Clifton College, although this was illegal. The chapel was not licensed for burials.

The school has welcomed a number of royal visitors, but the first one must have been an embarrassment to all concerned. Prince Albert Victor, second in line to the throne, was in the city to unveil a statue of his grandmother, Queen Victoria, on College Green. He had been persuaded to pass by

The statue of Earl Haig in the grounds (Janet Naylor)

the college and receive a deputation at its gates. In the event it rained, and the prince arrived late. He moved on after hearing only the start of a formal welcome being read to him.

By tradition it seems that every public school has to have its own song and Clifton is no exception. One of its 'old boys', the poet Sir Henry Newbolt, wrote the lyrics of 'The Best School of All' with music provided by Sir Hubert Parry, best-known for his choral work *Jerusalem*.

Other well-known former pupils include Lord Roberts, British Commander-in-Chief of the Forces in the Boer War and Earl Haig, Field Marshall in the First World War. A statue of Haig, cast in bronze, stands in the school grounds, although apparently it didn't fully meet with Lady Haig's approval. She thought the sculptor had failed to capture the chin of the man she knew so well.

Sir Arthur-Quiller-Couch, who edited the *Oxford Book of English Verse* and actors Sir Michael Redgrave, Trevor Howard and John Cleese also feature amongst Clifton's alumni.

After 125 years of being a boys' only school, Clifton College admitted girls to its sixth form in 1987 and is now fully co-educational.

⚓ SCHOOL FOR STARS ⚓

It was a touch of theatrical serendipity that led to one of the country's best-known stage schools getting a new home.

Bristol Old Vic's Theatre School began life in 1946 in cramped conditions in a building behind the stage door of the Theatre Royal in King Street. It was affectionately known as the 'fruit school' due to its closeness to the fruit and vegetable markets that then surrounded the theatre. Larger premises were needed, but the cost of buying and converting two rambling Victorian houses on the edge of Clifton Downs was prohibitive at the time. The purchase of the property was later achieved through a highly successful musical that had been written in-house and attracted large audiences both in this country and overseas.

It was written especially for the theatre school by Julian Slade, who in earlier days had been one of its students, along with actress Dorothy Reynolds. The couple had already collaborated on a production called *Christmas in King Street*. Slade, who at the time was Musical Director of the Bristol Old Vic Theatre Company, composed the music while Reynolds wrote the lyrics.

They called their new musical *Salad Days*, taking the title from a speech by by Cleopatra in Shakespeare's *Antony and Cleopatra*: 'My salad days, when I was green in judgment, cold in blood …' Slade and Reynolds intended the show to be a summer production, but it became an instant success with theatregoers and ran and ran.

The musical was given its world premiere in King Street early in the summer of 1954. It transferred in August to London's West End, where it ran for more than five years, or 2,283 performances. It became the longest-running show in musical theatre until overtaken by *My Fair Lady* in America in 1956 and *Oliver!* in this country in 1960. The musical went on to achieve enormous – though totally unexpected – success, with extended runs in Canada and on Broadway. Proceeds from the box-office takings allowed the theatre school to take over the houses in Downside Road and hire workmen to convert them. The new school was officially opened in 1956 by Dame Sybil Thorndike.

Since then the school has been a launchpad for the careers of some of Britain's best-known acting talent, including Amanda Redman, Jane Lapotaire, Helen Baxendale, Stephanie Cole, Greta Scacchi, the late Pete Postlethwaite, Jeremy Irons and Brian Blessed. Another former student, Daniel Day-Lewis, made Oscar history in 2013 by becoming the first man to win the Best Actor award three times.

Apart from those who walk in the front of the footlights, the school has also trained many designers, directors, prop makers and stage managers. Many of the students have also trod the boards of the Theatre Royal itself, the oldest working playhouse in the country; the curtain first went up in 1766.

☙ SEVEN STARS ANTI-SLAVERY ROLE ❧

An unpretentious one-bar pub, hidden down an alley and dwarfed by Bristol's first multi-storey office block, built in the 1960s, played a major role in the abolition of slavery.

It was here, at the Seven Stars in St Thomas Lane, that Thomas Clarkson, the son of a vicar and a Cambridge-educated clergyman himself, arrived in 1787 to collect information about the trade which was legal at the time but today is viewed with much abhorrence.

By the middle of the eighteenth century, Bristol had become a leading trade port in Europe and was also notorious for its involvement in the slave trade. Slaves were captured on the west coast of Africa and taken to work on plantations in America and the Caribbean in exchange for such things as trinkets, sugar and tobacco. Records show that between 1697 and 1807 more than 2,100 known ships left Bristol for the journey to pick up the slaves.

The landlord of the Seven Stars was sympathetic to the anti-slavery campaign and welcomed Thomas Clarkson. He was able to introduce him to disgruntled sailors who had worked on slave ships and showed Clarkson around some of the dockside pubs that helped to recruit for the trade. Despite the city's involvement in slavery, very few slaves actually came to the city and there is no historical evidence for the claims that are made from time to time, such as the rumour that slaves were held in chains in the crypts of various churches, including St Mary Redcliffe, and the nearby Redcliffe caves.

As so much of Bristol's money was tied up with the trade, Clarkson risked life and limb in being in the city. Many of his meetings had to take place under the cover of darkness. During his inquiries he collected equipment used on the slave ships such as iron handcuffs, leg shackles and branding irons. He passed all this, along with the information he had gathered, to his friend William Wilberforce, the Member of Parliament for Hull, who was one of the parliamentary leaders against the slave trade. A parliamentary bill for the abolition of the trade eventually received Royal Assent in 1807 and slavery itself was banned throughout the British Empire a quarter of a century later. Clarkson then published his book, *History of the Abolition of the African Slave Trade*. It included much of his research at the Seven Stars. A colourful plaque with a portrait of Clarkson is on the front of the Seven Stars, recording his visit.

❧ SHEEP GRAZING IN THE CITY ❧

Should you see sheep grazing on the Downs, do not be fooled into thinking that this beauty spot has been turned over to farmland. The sheep are nibbling the grass to help maintain an ancient but little-known valuable right.

Clifton and Durdham Downs, a vast expanse of open grassland and wooded country bordered on one side by the Avon Gorge, were originally the commons of two medieval manors adjoining each other. About 300 years ago, this was a dangerous and desolate area, frequented by highwaymen and footpads. A gibbet, where the bodies of murderers were left twisting in the wind, stood at the highest point of the Downs. This was the grim but aptly named Gallows Acre Lane, now known as Pembroke Road.

One of the most notorious of killers who lurked about the Downs was Shenkin Protheroe, an ill-formed dwarf with long and extra powerful arms. He ingratiated himself with kind-hearted passing travellers, who he would then grab by the throat and rob. On one occasion his victim died as a result of the attack. Protheroe was eventually caught, executed for murder, and hung on the gibbet.

In May 1861, both Clifton and Durdham Downs were secured for the citizens as a total of 442 acres of recreation land. This came about through the passing of an Act of Parliament prosaically titled the Clifton and Durdham Downs (Bristol) Act 1861. It stated that the Downs 'shall ever hereafter be kept open and unenclosed as a place of public resort'. Prior to the Act, Durdham Downs belonged to the lords of the manor of Henbury, while Clifton was in the hands of the Society of Merchant Venturers, an organisation which appears to have evolved from a thirteenth-century Guild of Merchants and still exists.

The method of looking after this beauty spot was also set up by the Act of Parliament. An equal number of city councillors and Merchant Venturers, who make up the Downs Committee, meet regularly to discuss day-to-day management. One thing that overrides all other rules is the right to graze sheep on the Downs, first granted in an Anglo-Saxon charter of AD 883. The right still exists for nineteen commoners, who include individuals, several schools on the edge of the Downs and the University of Bristol. In some cases, the right came to the present owners by way of a property acquisition, and in others, it was inherited. The Act of Parliament states that as long as the Downs remains a common – and sheep grazing is one legal proof of that – the land cannot be built upon. It prevents any encroachment of the area by property developers or speculative businessmen. So, from time to time the Commoners put out sheep on the grassland. Grazing can take place on Durdham Downs, but not Clifton.

The university is probably now the only commoner owning sheep. They are taken to the Downs from the farm at its veterinary school at Langford, Somerset, for the grazing ceremony.

At one time, more than 2,000 sheep roamed the Downs under the eye of a flockmaster, and they were taken to a yard at the back of a pub in Westbury-on-Trym village to be sheared. However, this pastoral scene did not bring joy to the hearts of everyone. The manager of the Clifton Down Hotel, now a block of apartments, complained that the noise of bleating sheep in the early hours of the morning disturbed his guests.

It was not complaints of noise that brought an end to large-scale grazing, however, but an outbreak of sheep scab in 1924.

⅚ SHIPSHAPE AND BRISTOL FASHION ⅔

Surprisingly for a city whose history and economy has been closely linked with the sea for 1,000 years, Bristol seems to have largely forgotten one of its sons who became passionate about improving the working conditions for seamen.

A plaque recording the birthplace of Samuel Plimsoll is so high up on the wall of a house in Redcliffe that passers-by can be forgiven for not seeing it. Plimsoll was born in Colston Parade, overlooking the south churchyard of St Mary Redcliffe in 1824. His home was just yards from Redcliffe Wharf, which in his childhood would have been packed with ships from around the world loading and unloading their cargoes. It may well be that memories of the wharf later influenced Plimsoll's thinking in maritime affairs.

He had an unusual career path, starting work as a clerk with a firm of solicitors and then moving on to manage a brewery. Plimsoll later became

Honorary Secretary of the Great Exhibition at Crystal Palace in 1851, a showcase for the country's scientific, cultural, industrial and engineering skills.

Plimsoll was elected Member of Parliament for Derby in 1868 and held the seat for twelve years. During this time he made a name for himself campaigning for better conditions for seamen. He published a document in 1872 entitled 'Our Seamen – An Appeal'. It showed that a large proportion of sailors in the merchant service who perished at sea lost their lives from preventable causes such as overloading of ships.

In parliament, Plimsoll initiated and carried through almost single-handedly what became the Merchant Act of 1876. This was aimed at improving the conditions for seamen working on overloaded and undermanned ships. Plimsoll's Act made it compulsory for all owners of ships to show a safety loading line on the side of their vessels. This soon became known as the Plimsoll line. Ships could

Samuel Plimsoll's statue on the quayside (Author's collection)

be loaded until they floated in the water at a line corresponding with expected conditions. By doing this, the ship should be safe on the high seas.

For many years a bust of Plimsoll on a plinth, engraved with his shipping safety line, was stored in a warehouse, although it had earlier stood on the dockside. Local campaigners helped to ensure it was returned and now Plimsoll's bust looks out across the floating harbour at Hotwells. It is a reminder of a man who was given the sobriquet 'the sailor's friend'.

⚜ SPRINGS AND SPAS ⚜

Stroll the streets of Hotwells, blighted by the main A4 road slicing the district into two parts with traffic thundering along all day and night, and you will be hard put to discern that this was once a fashionable spa. It ranked in the eighteenth century as one of the favourite resorts of the nobility and fashionable society, along with the spa at Bath.

Amongst those who wrote about the Hotwells spa or visited it were the writer Joseph Addison, the poets William Cowper and Alexander Pope and the playwright Richard Sheridan. Catherine of Braganza, the queen consort of Charles II, was also a visitor. The English poet William Whitehead was so impressed by the spa that he wrote 'A Hymn to the Nymph of the Bristol Spring'.

John Wesley, the founder of Methodism, is said to have taken the water at Hotwells. One of the spa's lessees in 1755 issued a pamphlet claiming that it was only after 'drinking at the well that the evangelist was sufficiently restored from a greedy consumption to undertake his tour of Devon and Cornwall'.

Lady Henrietta Hope left a permanent mark on the city when she visited the spa in 1785. She founded Hope Chapel, on nearby Hope Chapel Hill, which two centuries later is still being used for prayer and praise, as well as a community centre. Unfortunately, she died of consumption and never saw her chapel completed.

The spa's water emerged from a spring on the bank of the River Avon near St Vincent's Rock, at 60 gallons a minute. It became so popular that it was bottled and sold in the capital. An advertisement in one London newspaper read: 'Famous Bristol Hotwell water, fresh from the well, delivered to any part of the town for six shillings per dozen bottles.'

The traveller and writer Celia Fiennes described the water as 'warm as new milk and much of that sweetness'. One day in 1755, no one partook of the waters as they had turned red, apparently as a result of an earthquake in Lisbon. Word quickly spread that the spa water could cure a catalogue of diseases including gout, diabetes and consumption (tuberculosis). One doctor recommended a visit to Hotwells for people with 'hot livers, feeble brains and pimply faces'. It may well have been that the efficacious values of the spa were somewhat over-egged, for some visitors were taken ill and died. They were buried in the Strangers' Burial Ground at the foot of Clifton Hill.

For thirty years William Pennington was Master of Ceremonies at the spa. He had responsibility for arranging grand balls, entertainments and other amusements for visitors. Besides the Pump Room, which overlooked the River Avon, there were two large public rooms, where breakfast was served and country dances and balls held. A curving row of shops known as The Colonnade was built to serve the needs of visitors. The popularity of the spa also saw the inevitability of property speculators cashing in, by building lodging houses on the hills rising up to Clifton.

The Colonnade, the only reminder of the Hotwells spa (Trevor Naylor)

Hotwells spa's decline was almost as fast as its rise. The Pump Room and Hotwell House were demolished and the traders moved out of The Colonnade, although the building still exists and is the only reminder of the spa.

None of this put off the entrepreneur George Newnes from opening the Clifton Grand Spa and Hydro next to his Clifton Rocks Railway, however. He piped water from the Hotwells spring some 240ft through the rocks to his pump room.

Newnes' spa was soon given the civic seal of approval, with an official opening by the Mayoress of Bristol. It was described as a place where 'health-giving' spa water was dispensed; hence the inscription 'Aquam Bibe' (Drink Water) on the wall. Patrons could also enjoy lunchtime concerts.

A local paper described the pump room as being of 'admirable proportions, one hundred feet by fifty-seven feet which was elegant and light'. There were twenty columns of Cipolliono marble, a variety of marble used by the Ancient Greeks and the Romans. All the doors, window frames, panelling and floor were made of oak and in the centre of the room was a fountain of white marble with a raised fluted basin.

The directors boasted that it was the 'most highly decorated and finest' pump room in the United Kingdom. However, by 1922 the popularity of the spa had waned, and the pump room was turned into a cinema. That failed too, though, and eventually became a ballroom.

Another spring was discovered on Sion Hill in Clifton towards the end of the eighteenth century. The owner of a lodging house bored through the limestone rock until he reached hot water. He then built a pump room on top, but his venture proved to be unprofitable. The spring still proved useful, however: by 1811 it was supplying water to 300 homes nearby. Iron traps, which can still be seen in the pavements of Caledonia Place, once gave access to cisterns, where residents stored their water.

When the Bristol Waterworks Company was founded in 1846, its directors bought Sion Spring for £13,500. The St Vincent's Rocks Hotel was later built on the site of the pump room, but closed in 2004 with the building being converted into new homes.

𝒯

⋆ A TALL STORY ⋆

Giants, dwarves and fat ladies have appeared in travelling fairs and circuses in England since the 1600s. They were once big attractions as sideshows, with people flocking to stare at these unusual examples of human nature.

Patrick Cotter O'Brien was known as 'the Bristol Giant', on account of being over 8ft tall. He arrived in Bristol in the eighteenth century, having been brought to the city from his native Kinsale, County Cork, by a showman. O'Brien travelled to fairs all over England, initially earning about £50 a year.

He weighed 25 stones and wore size 15 shoes. It was said that O'Brien could eat twenty eggs and three loaves of bread at one meal. He needed two double beds in which to sleep. One newspaper reported that O'Brien could lean out of the first floor window of his lodgings and kiss women as they passed by. Another of his gimmicks was to light his pipe by lifting the lid off the oil lamps, which then lit the streets.

Patrick retired from the fairground circuit when he was 44 years old and then spent much time socialising at his local alehouse in Hotwells. The landlord provided him with a mahogany chair, which had a 27in wide seat. Sadly, O'Brien enjoyed only two years of retirement before dying of a lung and liver disease. He made arrangements for his own funeral, because he did not want medical researchers from the hospital exhuming his body for anatomical research. O'Brien left detailed instructions, stating that he should be buried in a wooden coffin sealed with lead, which would be put inside another box. It was to be buried 12ft below ground, with iron bars on top and set in rock.

At his funeral in 1806, O'Brien was still attracting crowds of sightseers. Some 2,000 people packed the roads around the Roman Catholic cemetery in Trenchard Street near the city centre, although the funeral was at 6 a.m. A hearse large enough to take his coffin could not be found, so fourteen pallbearers were recruited to carry it to the graveside in relays.

Twenty years later, builders who were digging the foundations for a new school accidentally discovered O'Brien's coffin with its nameplate still legible. Despite his wish, a surgeon was given permission to exhume O'Brien's body, examine it in the cause of medical research and reinter it afterwards. Medical opinion was that O'Brien's extraordinary height was due to his suffering from acromegaly, or gigantism, resulting from a defect in his pituitary glands.

After O'Brien's death, items of his clothing became valuable souvenirs. The pub chair he used, which had long disappeared, turned up at an auction house in 1969 and fetched £2,000.

Another Bristol resident advertised herself as the world's fattest woman. As a 12 year old, Lucy Moore weighed more than 27 stone. By adulthood, she was 48 stone, although she was only 5ft 4in tall. Lucy was born in Kentucky, USA, of mixed-race parents but came to England and settled on Constitution Hill, which steeply rises from Hotwells to Clifton.

By her mid-teens she was already well known for exhibiting herself on the stage, at fairgrounds and circuses. She adopted the stage name of 'The Jersey Lily', which also happened to be the nickname of Lillie Langtry, a mistress of the Prince of Wales (later Edward VII).

When Lucy died at the age of 43 in the Bristol Royal Infirmary in 1920, suffering from cancer, hundreds of people gathered outside the hospital's mortuary door. They jostled each other for space to see the coffin being put into the funeral hearse. Eight pallbearers were needed to carry it. Many hundreds of people also lined the route to Arnos Vale Cemetery where Lucy was buried, under her real name of Eliza Moore.

❖ TIME FOR CHANGE ❖

The notice that Daniel Burges, Town Clerk of Bristol, had published in the *Bristol Times* in September 1852 caused something of a stir in the city. It read:

> The existence of two records of time, from the inconvenience to which it exposes travellers, and the uncertainty of confusion it causes in the regulation of local engagements, is an evil. That the opinion of this council, it is desirable that the authorities having charge of the public clocks, should follow the practice adopted in other places, and regulate their clocks by Greenwich time only.

This announcement caused John Allis, who described himself on his invoices as 'watch, chronometer, hall and turret clock manufacturer', to tell his customers that he 'would feel obliged if the Ladies and Gentlemen, and public institutions where clocks and dials are wound and regulated by me, will intimate to me their wishes on the subject'. They were asked to contact Mr Allis at his premises in Albion Chambers, the passageway running between Broad Street and Small Street.

In the early Victorian period, Bristol was in two minds about the correct time. Although we now take Greenwich Mean Time or British Summer Time for granted, in those days no standard time existed in Bristol. Every city had its own local time, reckoned by the sun and signed by church bells. Bristol lies 2 degrees and 36 minutes west of the Greenwich Meridian, and so the sun reaches its noon peak eleven minutes later than Greenwich.

Before the growth of the railways, most people expected to spend their lives close to home. For Bristolians, this was about to change when the first through train from London pulled into Temple Meads station in 1841. The Great Western Railway began to tempt people to travel. They could get to London in hours, as opposed to days by stagecoach. If they wanted to catch a train at noon from Temple Meads, though, they had to remember that it would pull away from the platform at 11.49 a.m. Bristol Time.

To help Bristolians catch their train on time, Bristol Corporation arranged for the main public clock on the façade of the Exchange in Corn Street to show both local and Greenwich Mean Time. An extra second hand was fitted to the face of the clock to show the local time. The city finally adopted Greenwich Mean Time in 1852, but the Exchange clock still shows local time as well.

The clock on the façade of the Exchange
(Author's collection)

Behind the Exchange, another interesting and unusual timepiece can be found on the 205ft-high spire of St Nicholas church, overlooking Bristol Bridge. It is the only church clock in Britain to have an inset dial showing seconds. The clock was installed in the early nineteenth century and, for some unknown reason, the second hand was added during renovation in the 1870s.

In medieval times, the traditional curfew bell was sounded at St Nicholas' at 9 p.m. for two minutes every night, warning travellers outside the old city that St Nicholas Gate was about to close. Like many city centre churches, St Nicholas was devastated by fire during an air raid during the Bristol Blitz. The clock's mechanism was destroyed but later repaired. The original clock face is now run by an electric mechanism.

In neighbouring Broad Street, every quarter of an hour, brightly painted quarter-jacks high above the west door of Christ Church with St Ewen swing their hammers, striking two bells the appropriate number of times. These quaint timekeepers were carved in 1728 by well-known Bristol architect Thomas Paty. They were taken down nearly sixty years later when the church was demolished for road widening and a new one built. But the quarter-jacks weren't put back until the early 1900s. They had been in the safekeeping of a local antiquarian for over 100 years. At regular intervals the quarter-jacks are removed for maintenance and to have their uniforms repainted.

Chris Church's other claim to fame is that its baptismal register contains the name of one Robert Southey, Poet Laureate from 1813 until his death in 1843. He was born around the corner from the church, in Wine Street.

⁓ TOBACCO TOWERS ⁓

Three red- and blue-brick tower blocks that stand majestically near the entrance to the floating harbour at Cumberland Basin are testimony to an industry that was a major player in the local economy for several centuries. The original use of the purpose-built nine-storey bonded warehouses was to store tobacco under supervision of the Customs and Excise until duty was paid.

Former tobacco bonds (Trevor Naylor)

It's not generally realised that until the seventeenth century, tobacco was a banned import in Bristol. Merchants in London enjoyed a monopoly of the tobacco trade until 1639, when the Privy Council of Charles I revoked a long-standing order that tobacco should be shipped only to the Port of London. Despite this, the Cumberland Basin bonded warehouses, built with reinforced concrete, were not constructed until over 200 years later – between 1905 and 1909 – by the Bristol-based family firm of William Cowlin. They were erected at a time when there was a boom in imports of tobacco.

The vast number of soldiers serving on the Western Front in the First World War were supplied with cigarettes and when they returned home they kept up the smoking habit. By the late 1960s, more than 20 per cent of the total imports of tobacco into the United Kingdom passed through the Port of Bristol.

Tobacco leaf was imported from East Africa, India and Canada as well as the USA. When it arrived at Avonmouth Docks, casks packed with leaf were taken by barge and road to the bonded warehouses. It was only released from these fortress-like buildings by Customs and Excise officers on payment of duty by the cigarette manufacturers. Casks were stored on each of the nine floors at the Cumberland Basin warehouses.

There were more tobacco bonds at Canons Marsh, in the centre of the city. These were demolished in 1988 to make way for new administrative headquarters of a bank. This became the catalyst of the dockside regeneration that is still going on. Taken altogether, the bonds could hold more than 150,000 casks of tobacco leaf.

As health awareness grew, however, the demand for tobacco products started to fall. By 1999, the largest of the tobacco manufacturers in Bristol, W.D. & H.O. Wills, had closed their factories in the city. In its heyday, the firm employed 6,000 people locally.

B Bond, the oldest of the Cumberland Basin warehouses, is now home to the archives of the Bristol Records Office and also accommodates the Create Centre, which promotes environmental awareness. C Bond has been converted to provide individual storage units.

❧ UNUSUAL PUB ACTIVITIES ❧

It's not only in modern times that pub landlords have run promotional campaigns aimed at luring more customers into their bars. In 1827, the landlord of the Star Inn at Cannon Street in Bedminster (now known as the Steam Crane Alehouse) certainly had a novel idea, but unfortunately it led to a shocking tragedy.

He bought a lion from a man he met on the dockside and put it on show – in its cage – in the garden of his pub. It attracted many new customers and the landlord, encouraged by this increase in trade, decided to go a stage further with

Not your usual pub feature (SXC)

his stunt. He hired a man by the name of Joseph Kiddle to spend some time with the animal in its cage. The inevitable happened and within seconds Mr Kiddle was mauled to death. This tragic incident was featured in a play written and produced locally in 1974.

The Revd Emmanuel Collins, landlord of another pub in Bedminster in the eighteenth century, was in the news for a totally different reason. To augment his income as a clergyman, he conducted marriage ceremonies at his pub, The Sign of the Duke of Marlborough. This was, of course, illegal.

⁘ VANBRUGH'S BRISTOL HOUSE ⁘

Bristol is the only city outside London that has a building designed by the celebrated eighteenth-century architect, Sir John Vanbrugh. His Kings Weston House is a hidden treasure, for it cannot be seen by passing travellers. It stands in grounds of about 300 acres, with panoramic views across the Severn Estuary to the distant Welsh Hills and down to the Somerset coast.

Sir John is, of course, well known for designing Blenheim Palace in Oxfordshire, and Castle Howard, of *Brideshead Revisited* fame, in Yorkshire. He was commissioned in about 1712 by Edward Southwell who, like his father, was a Member of Parliament for Bristol.

Kings Weston House (Kings Weston Action Group)

Kings Weston House stands on the site of a Tudor mansion that Sir Robert Southwell bought in 1679, due to it being equidistant between his family estates in Kinsale, Ireland, and court in London. It was reported by the *Gloucester Journal* in 1739 that Edward Southwell, who enjoyed entertaining guests, employed a baker, a butcher and two brewers to provide for 'all-comers' at his house. Most of the food was 'produced on the estate'. William III was entertained here in 1690, on his return from his victory at the Battle of the Boyne. The king's ship anchored off Avonmouth and he was brought up the River Avon in a smaller boat, to disembark at a spot near the present Lamplighters public house.

The Tudor manor remained standing, as the present house was progressively built around it, replacing the old wings with new. Among the distinctive features that Vanbrugh included is an unusual arcade of chimneys, as well as a roof that also incorporated a lookout platform, from where the family could watch the shipping in the Severn Estuary.

Kings Weston House has one of the most significant collections of Vanbrugh buildings around the estate – the Loggia, the Brewhouse, the Echo, Kingsweston Inn (which has been much altered) and Penpole Lodge, now standing in ruins. Other buildings, like the existing stable block and Shirehampton Lodge, today the entrance to a golf club, were added later by another architect, Robert Mylne.

Kings Weston House remained in the Southwell family until 1838, when it was sold to Philip John Miles of Leigh Court Estate in North Somerset. He bought it so that the family of his second wife would have an inheritance, whilst that of his first inherited Leigh Court.

The last of the Miles family, Philip Napier Miles, was a composer and musician and became friends with another composer, Ralph Vaughan Williams. It was at Kings Weston that Williams completed his classical work *The Lark Ascending*, which was given its premiere at nearby Shirehampton Public Hall in 1920. It is now one of Britain's favourite pieces of music. Another Vaughan Williams composition, Kings Weston, is less well known.

Kings Weston House stayed in the ownership of the Miles family until 1935, when Philip Napier Miles died, aged 70. He had no heir, so the house was sold to pay death duties.

Since then, the mansion has had a somewhat chequered history. During the Second World War, it was used as a transit camp for troops. Afterwards, more than 500 primary school children moved into its grand rooms for their lessons, while permanent schools were being built on the nearby Lawrence Weston estate. Kings Weston House later became a school of architecture. Then, in 1970, Bristol Corporation bought it for £305,000, with the help of a Home Office grant. Kings Weston then became a police training school, but twenty-five years later, the police constables and detectives moved out, into purpose-built headquarters at Portishead.

Family portraits in the Oak Room, Kings Weston House (Kings Weston Action Group)

Kings Weston House, which originally stood in Gloucestershire, but is now well within the Bristol city boundary, is privately owned once again. Much of the estate is now a public park, managed by the city council.

❖ A VILLAGE DESTROYED FOR NOTHING ❖

It was the quintessential picture postcard English village. About thirty-eight houses, a post office, village hall, infant school, a common, several farmhouses and a duck pond – which seems to be obligatory if the village is to appear on the cover of a chocolate box.

There was a saddler too, who repaired harnesses and boots. After a day working on the farm or in the orchards, the menfolk of the village could quench their thirst in the Carpenters Arms.

The people who lived at Charlton, on the northern fringe of Bristol, were proud of their history, which could be traced back to Anglo-Saxon times. It was the sort of village where everyone knew each other and little, if anything, newsworthy happened. But Charlton was propelled into the national headlines when the House of Lords made a shock announcement in 1946: the village would have to be demolished. It was to make way for the building – by the

Bristol Aeroplane Company – of what at the time would be the world's biggest aircraft. The homes of the Charlton villagers would have to be bulldozed, to be replaced by a runway 2,300 yards long – long enough for the new plane, called the Brabazon, to take off and land.

All thirty families at Charlton protested, but without success. They were promised by the government that another village would be built nearby, but it never was. Compulsory Purchase Orders were issued to each property owner and most of the people of Charlton were moved into homes on the nearby council estate of Patchway. All they could do was to watch helplessly as the rubble from their homes was buried under 15ft of soil and tarmac.

The Bristol type 176 Brabazan, as it was called on the drawing board, was a propeller-driven aircraft designed by the Bristol Aeroplane Company to fly 100 passengers from London to New York, non-stop. It would fly at a cruising speed of 300mph.

The 'Brab' as it became known, was 50ft high with a wing span of 230ft and a length of 177ft. The cockpit alone contained more than 1,000 instrument dials. Well over 1,000 aircraft workers who had been employed on the project watched in awe as the Brabazon took off on its maiden flight in September 1949. Bill Pegg, the Bristol Aircraft Corporation's chief test pilot, was at the controls. A crowd of 20,000 people watched as he took the plane into skies above Bristol and Gloucestershire. It later made demonstration flights at the Farnborough International Air Show.

By the time the aircraft had made its maiden flight, £3 million had been spent on the Brabazon project. But it was already out of date. In fact not one airline had placed an order for it. For political and financial reasons, the government announced in 1953 that the Brabazon would be scrapped, having never made a commercial flight. Altogether £12 million of the taxpayer's money had been spent on it.

The Brabazon's hangar later became the home of the production line for the world's first supersonic aircraft, the Anglo–French Concorde. Only twenty planes, six for development and fourteen for commercial use, were built before that project was scrapped, too.

Meanwhile, the name Charlton survives in the name of a road near the old village and in the title of several nearby housing developments. But it seems that the villagers of Charlton lost their homes for nothing.

❧ WALKING BY WATER ❧

Little could Lord Robert de Berkeley have envisaged that his gift of water in 1190 to the growing hamlet of Redcliffe would be remembered more than 800 years later in one of Bristol's most unusual annual customs. It sees the vicar of St Mary Redcliffe church, picking his way around cabbage patches, peering down manholes and bumping his flock on mini tombstones.

Lord de Berkeley, who was Lord of the Manor of Bedminster, gave the priest and inhabitants of Redcliffe a supply of water from his 'ruge', or ridge well, on a hilltop at Knowle, just under 2 miles south of the church. This was the only source of fresh water for the people of Redcliffe for 500 years and it is the oldest known gift to the church, but it was typical of the endowments of the time.

In those days the city was supplied by the rivers Frome and Avon. They were used for supplying drinking water as well as the disposal of sewage. Such unsanitary conditions led to outbreaks of cholera and typhoid, so Lord de Berkeley's gift must have been more than welcome.

A lease dated 14 July 1566 makes provision for a branch pipe, known as a 'feather of water,' to take the supply from the church on to the hospital of St John the Baptist. This stood on the site of the existing traffic roundabout beside the church, but at the time it went by the rather insalubrious name of Redcliffe Pit. The hospital authorities were required each year on St John the Baptist's Day – 24 June – to pay the Proctors of Redcliffe and their successors 12*d*, if lawfully required, as 'a knowledge of a rent or duty for the holding of the said feather of water'. Every autumn the vicar of St Mary Redcliffe, along with the churchwardens and parishioners, take part in a trek that down the years has become known as the Pipe Walk. This enables the church to lay claim to certain endowments and maintain a right of way.

The walk starts at the well head, sited in the midst of a large field of allotments at Knowle and takes in pastureland, public footpaths and even a private garden. It is the vicar's duty to inspect manholes to ensure that the pipe is still there. After crossing the busy St John's Lane, the walkers head into Victoria Park, where it is customary for the vicar, helped by the churchwardens, to ceremoniously bump first-time 'pipe-walkers' on a stone tablet, rather like a small tombstone.

The water maze in Victoria Park (Author's collection)

A bronze water outlet at St Mary Redcliffe church (Author's collection)

Water has not run the full length of the pipe for some years, but since 1984, it has flowed into a fountain in Victoria Park that is built of brick and is designed as a maze. It is notable for having no dead ends, and it is a replica of one of the 2,000 medieval roof bosses in St Mary Redcliffe church. The boss must be the smallest maze in the country, measuring just 4in in diameter.

The Pipe Walk ends at a bronze water outlet, underneath the balustraded promenade running alongside the church. A Latin inscription, roughly translated, reads, 'For the health of the soul of Robert de Berkeley, who gave to God and to the church of St Mary Redcliffe and its ministers the Rugewell and its conduit'.

In the early part of the twentieth century, the Pipe Walk was a rather grand affair. The *Western Daily Press* reported that those who walked the route were treated to a dinner in a marquee with music provided by a band. The newspaper report noted that the church authorities thought that 'people who had trouble for a long walk should benefit of a comfortable refection afterwards'. These days, the walkers are more likely to get a cup of coffee and a piece of cake, but they are still as grateful as ever to Lord de Berkeley for his gift of water.

❧ WAR RUBBLE GOES TO THE STATES ❧

With Bristol being the fifth most heavily bombed city in Britain during the Second World War, the city fathers not only had the problem of redevelopment to deal with, but also that of disposing the many hundreds of thousands of tons of rubble. During the Bristol Blitz – from November 1940 until the following May – there were seventy-seven air raids, six of them classified as major. Altogether, 1,299 people were killed and another 3,305 injured. During the entire war, more than 3,000 of Bristol's houses were destroyed and nearly 100,000 properties damaged.

The first great blitz came on 24 November 1940, changing the face of the city forever. Many public buildings, including churches, the main shopping centre which stood on what is now Castle Park, offices and homes were reduced to mini-mountains of twisted girders, burning timbers, bricks and plasterwork. City officials faced with the mammoth task of getting all this cleared away came up with an innovative answer to the problem facing them, though.

The ruins of some of the bombed buildings went to the United States of America as ballast in ships that had brought much-needed supplies to Britain and were returning home empty. The debris was used as a foundation to build East River Drive in New York. In 1942, a plaque commemorating this unusual link between Bristol and America was unveiled at a special ceremony attended by British Marines and the Mayor of New York.

By the time work started on redeveloping the area in 1970, the plaque had disappeared. However, the English-Speaking Union stepped in when the redevelopment was completed four years later and organised a ceremony for a replacement plaque to be unveiled. It was dedicated by the Bristol-born Hollywood film star Cary Grant. The wording of the plaque reminds a new generation of the debt that all who hold freedom dear owe to those in Britain, who lost so much in its name. The people of Bristol have their own reminder of what must be an early form of recycling in a similar plaque in the city centre.

Part of a tramline embedded in the churchyard of St Mary Redcliffe (Author's collection)

An unusual reminder of the horrors of war stands in St Mary Redcliffe churchyard. Leaning at a precarious angle, but firmly embedded in the earth, is a section of tramline which had been lifted from the nearby road during a bombing raid and hurled several hundred yards over rooftops. It landed just a few yards from the church building itself.

Remarkably, as bombs rained down on the Redcliffe district, this iconic church escaped serious damage while buildings all around were reduced to rubble. Yet the church, with its cloud-piercing spire standing out between a main-line railway station and the docks, must have been a target for German bombers. Shortly after the air raid, Cannon Sydney Swann, vicar of St Mary Redcliffe, wrote:

> The tramline had come right over the doctor's house on the corner of Redcliffe Hill and Colston parade. How high it went into the air I have no idea. I remember thinking 'that tramline must remain. It will be of interest.

In the same air raid on Good Friday 1941, St Paul's church, barely half a mile away in Bedminster, was gutted with only its four walls left standing. Amazingly, 300 people who had taken shelter in the crypt later emerged unhurt. Some of them described this as a modern miracle.

One of the largest bombs dropped in the city during the war landed in Knowle. Measuring 8ft 11in long and weighing 4,000lbs, it created a crater about 30ft deep in the road. People living nearby showed that despite the rigours of war, they had not lost their sense of humour: they named the bomb 'Satan'. It was made safe and included in the London Victory parade in 1945.

❧ A 'WATERLOO' CHURCH FOR BRISTOL ❧

A triumphal mood swept the country after the Duke of Wellington's victory at the Battle of Waterloo in 1815, which ended the long wars with France. Army regiments, streets and village halls were named after him, statues of him were erected across the country and cities honoured the duke by granting him the Freedom of their boroughs.

When Wellington arrived in Bristol to accept the Freedom of the City, he was welcomed in grand style. A 'triumphal arch' was erected across Park Street for his horse-drawn carriage to pass through en route to the civic ceremony. Afterwards, the duke was guest of honour at a banquet hosted by the great and the good of the city.

Three years after the Battle of Waterloo, the government announced that it would be making £1 million available to build new churches. The Church Buildings Commission was founded to direct the distribution of the grant. Churches that benefited from the funding became known as 'Waterloo' or 'Commissioners' churches'. Some of the money came the way of the Diocese of Bristol which for some time had been considering the provision of church worship for people living around the Brandon Hill area. Hence, the construction of St George's church: Bristol's only 'Waterloo Church'.

Sir Robert Smirke, one of the three Crown architects who were instructed to prepare designs for the new churches around the country, was engaged to work on St George's. Here he was presented with the task of building a church on a steeply sloping site between two streets in the centre of the city. However, Smirke took the opportunity of making the southern approach to St George's a dramatic flight of forty-eight steps which ascended from Great George Street. It took two years for Sir Robert to complete the church, with its distinctive cupola and impressive portico supported by four Corinthian pillars. He built St George's with galleries on three sides that could seat 1,416 people; 500 of the seats were for renting out whilst the others were free.

The first services were held in 1823, and nine years later, St George's was made a parish church in its own right, having initially been a chapel of ease to the nearby St Augustine the Less. By the middle of the 1980s, the number of people being offered bread and communion wine had dwindled, largely as a result of the houses surrounding the church being converted from family homes into offices. The Church of England therefore declared St George's redundant as a place of worship.

A charitable trust was formed to turn the building into a recording and concert hall, where everything from folk to jazz, chamber concerts to classical music can be heard. The acoustics are such that the BBC is able to broadcast concerts from St George's, both live and recorded. A studio has been built in the crypt, which was once used by local people as an air-raid shelter during the Bristol Blitz.

WHALE ATTRACTS THE CROWDS

Littleton Pill in South Gloucestershire almost became a place of pilgrimage for two weeks in January 1885. It was not the arrival of a great religious leader that attracted crowds of people, though: a whale had beached there. Hundreds of visitors flocked to the inlet of the Severn Estuary to see the 66ft-long mammal, which weighed 50 tons. Such was the interest that a special train ran from Temple Meads, the main station in Bristol, to Thornbury, the nearest stop to Littleton Pill. A return ticket cost 1s 3d.

The whale had been washed ashore after swimming up the River Severn and trying to return to sea when it became stranded by the ebb tide. After two weeks, the smell of the dead mammal was so overpowering that it was towed downriver to Avonmouth. From there it was taken to St Philips in Bristol, where it was put on show. This time visitors were charged sixpence to see the whale before it was finally used as animal fertiliser.

WIGWAM FOR ARTISTS

In the garden of the Red Lodge, a Georgian house on Park Row run by Bristol Museum, stands one of the most unusual meeting places in the country. The so-called 'Wigwam', built along the lines of an old Gloucestershire barn, is the home of a group of artists.

It seems that they, perhaps more than other creative folk, need the comradeship of their fellows. To meet this need, Ernest Ehlers invited his 'brothers of the brush' to meet at his studio to work and talk. That was in 1894 and led to the setting up of a society known as the Bristol Savages. At first, they met in private studios, but since 1920 the Savages have been meeting in their Wigwam. They bought the building thanks to the generosity of their members and gave it to the city, on the condition that it would be their meeting place. At their weekly gatherings, the artists enjoy a sketching session on a subject chosen by the chairman of the night. Afterwards, their work is exhibited for inspection and informal discussion by fellow members.

Each 'Brother Savage' wears a lapel badge; the three types of members wear different coloured lapel feathers. Artists wear red, entertainers (from singers to raconteurs) wear blue, and lay members wear green. The feathers are held in a pin badge made from an American 5 cent piece with the head of Chief Johnny Big Tree on the coin. He was a guest of the Savages in the 1920s. Visitors to the Wigwam meetings are formally welcomed with a toast and a traditional Sioux greeting.

Each May, the Savages open the Wigwam to the public with their annual exhibition of work. Paintings on display include landscapes, seascapes and portraits. These are not the sketches made at the weekly meetings, but the result of many hours of painstaking work by the artists in their own studios. The paintings sell at prices ranging from a few hundred to several thousand pounds.

The Red Lodge was built in 1590 and is considered a rarity: a surviving sixteenth-century lodge house with the original interior. It has often been described as a national treasure. In 1854 the house was bought by Lady Bryon, widow of the poet, for Mary Carpenter, a pioneer of social reform. It was here that Miss Carpenter opened the first reformatory school in the country for girls. After the school closed in 1917, the Savages acquired the building.

⚘ WILD WEST COMES TO TOWN ⚘

Long before the invention of radio, television, video games and the Internet, families had to make do with homespun entertainment. They often gathered around the piano for a family sing-song, or simply talked to each other.

So when Buffalo Bill came to town with his Wild West Show, it was only natural that thousands of families would leave their homes to welcome him. William Frederick Cody, better known by his nickname of 'Buffalo Bill', had a great deal of life experience. He had herded cattle, worked on a wagon train, mined for gold, ridden the Pony Express, scouted for the army, fought in the American Civil War and even spent some time as a buffalo hunter.

Being something of an entrepreneur before the word came into everyday usage, he put together an amazing extravaganza of a travelling show about the Wild West. He took it on tour around America and Europe, taking in Bristol for just one visit. It was in September 1891 that Buffalo Bill and his entourage took the city by storm when they arrived at Temple Meads railway station. The touring show was so big that four goods trains arrived at hourly intervals, carrying the cast, animals and all the necessary props. As they disembarked, the cast and animals lined up for a carnival-style procession to their temporary camp. The thousands of spectators who lined the streets witnessed a spectacular sight as Native Americans, cowboys, stagecoaches and a herd of buffalo slowly made their way along the Gloucester Road to Horfield Common.

An army of workmen battled around the clock to erect a temporary stadium on the common in time for the first show two days later. The organisers of the show put on two performances every day for a week. Advertisements in the *Bristol Evening News* simply described the shows as 'representations of Indian and Frontier life'. They included a re-enactment of Custer's Last Stand, Native American attacks on a wagon train, daredevil riding and an appearance by American sharpshooter Annie Oakley. To provide musical accompaniment, Buffalo Bill brought with him a band of 250 musicians.

The Box Office was kept busy throughout the week as word of the shows spread around the city. Some 100,000 people bought a ticket priced at 1s for a seat in the stadium. When the final curtain came down Bristolians, it seems, couldn't get enough of the Wild West. They took to the streets once again, this time to wave farewell to the performers and animals as they returned to Temple Meads en route for their next venue. For a long time afterwards people living near Horfield Common referred to it as Buffalo Bill's Fields. The site was used by Clifton Rugby Club which played home matches there from 1893–96.

❧ ZOO GOES APE OVER NEW ANIMAL ❧

When one of the city's best-known residents died, there was much coverage about this in the national press. It was not that the deceased had led an adventurous or courageous life, but simply that he was a gorilla with a very large following.

Alfred was bought for £350 by Bristol in 1930 from the Congo, where his parents had been shot dead whilst raiding farmers' fields for food. When he arrived at the zoo, Alfred was then the only gorilla in captivity in this country. From the day of his arrival, he became extremely popular not only with his keepers but the thousands of visitors the zoo attracted each year. Alfred could often be seen walking around the grounds wearing his trademark woolly jumper, accompanied by one of his keepers. Many hundreds of picture postcards of him were sent around the world, some of them by American servicemen who were based at Clifton College around the corner during the Second World War. He even received greetings cards on 5 September each year, regarded by zoo staff as his birthday, although this was actually the day he had arrived at the zoo.

Alfred died in 1948, when he was thought to be 21 years old. Zoo officials announced that his death was caused by a low-flying aircraft, which made

Alfred the gorilla (Bristol Zoo Gardens)

Women racing at a fête, held at Bristol Zoo Gardens in the early twentieth century (Bristol Zoo Gardens)

him panic and collapse. It was kept quiet for some time that Alfred had actually been suffering from tuberculosis for a year. Such was his fame that taxidermists mounted his skin, which is still on display in the City Museum and Art Gallery. Alfred is also remembered at the zoo by a bronze cast of his head outside the Ape House.

The zoo was opened in 1836, after being founded by a group of prominent Bristolians, including members of the Wills tobacco and Fry's chocolate families. Isambard Kingdom Brunel was also an original subscriber. A site for the zoo was originally earmarked at Arnos Vale to the south-east of the city, but that became a cemetery instead. Eventually 12 acres of farmland on the edge of Clifton Downs became the zoo's home.

The zoo has long kept close contact with local hospitals. Indeed, surgeons from the Bristol Royal Infirmary have operated on sick animals and on one occasion two baby bears were admitted to the children's hospital, suffering from pneumonia.

In Victorian times its gardens became a focus for social and recreational occasions for visitors, as well as a place of natural history study. There were flower shows, performances by bands, tennis, croquet, archery and boat trips on the lake. One of the biggest attractions was a Bank Holiday appearance by the American tightrope walker Charles Blondin, who once crossed the Niagara Falls. His task at the zoo was far less arduous, though. The rope, 60ft high, was stretched 300ft across the lake. Admission fees for the event totalled £700, but half of this went to Blondin's agent.

Strangely, the lake was later chosen for the launching of two lifeboats. After the official ceremony one was taken by train to Lossiemouth in Scotland, while the other went to North Devon.

During the Second World War, some of the animals were moved from Clifton to places of safety, but the zoo never closed. However, its gardens were turned over to growing vegetables instead of flowers and the polar bear enclosure was converted into an air-raid shelter for the staff.

Also from The History Press

WHEN DISASTER STRIKES

Also from The History Press

HAUNTED

This series is sure to petrify everyone interested in the ghostly history of their hometown. Containing a terrifying collection of spine-chilling tales, from spooky sightings in pubs and theatres to paranormal investigations in cinemas and private homes, each book in the series is guaranteed to appeal to both serious ghost hunters and those who simply fancy a fright.

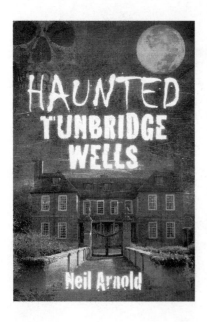

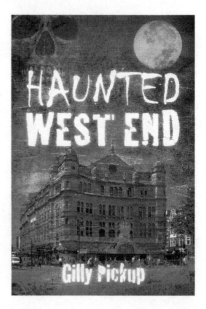

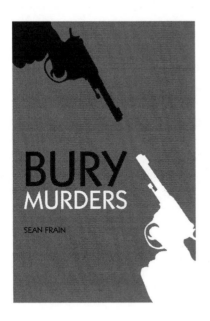